BIG BRANDS
BIG TROUBLE

BIG BRANDS
BIG TROUBLE

Lessons Learned
the Hard Way

JACK TROUT

JOHN WILEY & SONS, INC.

New York • Chichester • Weinheim • Brisbane • Singapore • Toronto

ISBN 0-471-41432-8

Printed in the United States of America.

10 9 8 7 6 5 4 3 2 1

This book is dedicated to the gentleman who has been bugging me to write on this subject for years. He'll remain anonymous to keep him out of trouble.

PREFACE

In recent years, business executives have been more in search of role models than ever before. Tom Peters probably gave this trend a giant boost with the very successful book he co-authored—*In Search of Excellence* (Harper & Row, 1982).

Excellence, as defined in that book, didn't equal longevity, however; many of the role models offered there have since foundered.

The book was based on a McKinsey research study of 75 highly regarded companies and involved extensive structured interviews as well as a 25-year literature review. To qualify as excellent, each top performer had to score well over the long haul in both growth and economic health. But not many years after this widely popular book was published, many of those excellent performers were in trouble, including companies like Digital Equipment, IBM, Data General, Kmart, and Kodak. In retrospect, a better title for the book might have been "In Search of Strategy."

The lessons that emerged were staples as traditional as motherhood and apple pie: Stay close to the customer; hold fast to the values of entrepreneurship; find productivity through people; be hands on and value driven; stick to your knitting. (You get the idea.) One of my favorite truisms was a "bias for action." A senior Digital Equipment Corporation executive was quoted thus, "When we've got a big problem here, we grab ten senior guys and stick them in a room for a week. They come up with the answer and implement it." But, it later turned out that they were coming up with the wrong answers. So much for the "ten guys in a room" lesson.

And later books by Tom Peters may not give you much more guidance either. As a *Fortune* article commented, "Because the more one talks to Peters, the more one recognizes that Peters, through the 1990s, has spent more and more time talking about gifted freaks, examples that are impossible to emulate" (November 13, 2000).

More recently, the popular method-by-example book has been *Built To Last* (HarperCollins, 1994), by James Collins and Jerry Porras. In it, they write glowingly about "Big Hairy Audacious Goals" that turned the likes of Boeing, Wal-Mart, General Electric, IBM, and others into the successful giants they have become.

The companies that the authors of *Built To Last* suggest for emulation were founded from 1812 (Citicorp) to 1945 (Wal-Mart). These firms didn't have to deal with the intense competition in today's global economy. While there is much you can learn from their success, they had the luxury of growing up when business life was a lot simpler. As a result, these role models are not very useful for companies today.

I have a better approach.

Not only is learning from failure easier, it offers a more thorough analysis of what works and what doesn't. We have always been taught that we should learn from our mistakes. Looking at the "downs" alongside the "ups" in the lives of the superbrands can show you what commonly goes wrong. There is no shortage of companies that recently have moved from glory days to difficult days.

Readers of my previous books may recognize some of the companies that form the case studies. While I've written about these companies before, this time around I put them under a microscope to draw out the underlying reasons for their difficulties and to suggest some things that could have been done to save them.

Within these stories, I describe some personal experiences for the first time. This isn't a tell-all book, but it uses candid analysis to help readers understand how easy it is for things to start down a road that puts a rich, successful company into big trouble.

And big trouble isn't easy to fix.

CONTENTS

BIG BRANDS
BIG TROUBLE

CHAPTER 1

The Most Popular Mistakes and Their High Cost

Long ago and far away, I started my career at General Electric. It was the early 1960s and, in hindsight, it was a wonderful time. Competition, as we know it, just didn't exist.

GE's main full-line competitor was a company called Westinghouse, but by today's standards, it was barely a real one. Westinghouse was a player, but GE actually saw the company more as a necessity. If that competition ever went away, the government would pounce on GE to break its hold on "electricity."

Back then, nobody really worried much about mistakes because CEOs figured they would be able to get any lost business back in the end. (Jack Welch hadn't yet arrived at GE. After he took over, everyone worried a lot more about mistakes.)

What's Changed

Today there are so many competitors that they quickly take your business if you make a mistake. Your chances of getting it back are slim unless someone else in turn makes a mistake. Hoping for competitors to make mistakes is like running a race with the hope that other racers will fall down. It isn't a very smart strategy.

Even worse is the large number of participants in each race. Every category is haunted by what I call the "tyranny of choice." Consumers have so many choices that one false step brings not just one, but an army of competitors to take advantage of your misstep. And what's especially tragic is that you don't get that business back. It's gone. (The General Motors story in Chapter 2 dramatizes this problem.)

In the following chapters, there are details about a lot of mistakes and the high cost that companies paid for making them. But before wheeling in the big brands, it is helpful to look at the most prevalent blunders in our hypercompetitive world and hint at the lessons they provide.

The "Me-too" Mistake

Many people believe that the basic issue in marketing is convincing the prospect that they have a better product or service. They say to themselves, "We might not be first but we're going to be better."

That may be true, but if you're late into a market space and have to do battle with large, well-established competitors, then your marketing strategy is probably faulty. Me-too just won't cut it.

Consider the efforts of Pepsi in the lemon-lime category. Even though supermarket soda aisles are overcrowded and sales growth is flat, Pepsi is launching Sierra Mist, a competitor to Sprite and 7UP. This is after two failed prior attempts (Slice and a product called "Storm").

Their introductory strategy is, what else, a "better" soda. Dawn Hudson, Pepsi's senior vice president of strategy and marketing, boasted in the *Wall Street Journal* that Sierra Mist will have a "cleaner, lighter, more refreshing lemon-lime."

Well, we'll have to see, but I wouldn't bet on its success as it sounds awfully "me-too" to me.

Another disadvantage of being a me-too is that the name of the first brand to market often becomes generic. Xerox, Kleenex, Coke, Scotch tape, Gore-Tex, Krazy Glue, and Q-tips all have an enormous advantage over competitive me-too products.

If the secret of success is getting into the prospective customer's mind first, which strategy are most companies committed to? The better-product strategy. Benchmarking is a popular subject in the business management field. Touted as the "ultimate competitive strategy," it involves comparing and evaluating your company's products against the best in the industry. It's an essential element in a process often called "total quality management" (TQM).

Benchmarking doesn't work because regardless of a product's objective quality, people perceive the first brand to enter their mind as superior. When you're a me-too, you're a second-class citizen. Marketing is a battle of perceptions, not products.

When you enter a market, a far better strategy is "Differentiation." Why are you different from the other players in the category? If you can define that difference in a meaningful way, you can escape the me-too trap. (How to do this is outlined in my book, *Differentiate or Die* [Wiley, 2000].)

The "What Are You Selling?" Mistake

This may surprise you, but I have spent a good bit of my time over the years figuring out exactly what people are trying to sell. Defining the product category in a simple, understandable way is essential.

Companies, large and small, often have a tough time describing their product, especially if it's a new category and a new technology.

Or else they describe the product in confusing terms that doom the effort right out of the gate.

The positioning of a product in the mind must begin with what the product is. We sort and store information by category. If you present a prospect with a confusing category, your chances of getting into his or her mind are slim to none.

What's a PDA?

Consider the problems that Apple encountered with the introduction of their Newton, a product they called a "PDA."

Immediately, their biggest positioning problem was: What are we selling?

The first print advertisements asked the question, "What is a Newton?" The television commercials asked the questions "What is a Newton? Where is a Newton? Who is a Newton?"

Apple, however, failed to answer these questions with words that users could comfortably absorb.

PDA, or "personal digital assistant," is not a category, nor is there much hope in its becoming one. (Pretty Damned Abstract is one tongue-in-cheek definition of PDA.)

Companies don't create categories. Users do. And so far, users haven't turned PDA into a category. Have you heard anyone ask another person about his or her PDA? It sounds like a medical problem. Even the trade press has landed on "Hand helds" as a generic term.

And you can't force the issue. Customers either are going to use your words or they aren't. If they don't, you have to give up and look for a new category name.

The Newton died, and the Palm, a simple, high-tech organizer has become a runaway success.

Articulating What You're Selling

When faced with the tough task of coming up with a name for what you're selling, start with a simple analysis of how the new product works, then try to use those words to describe it. When the automobile was born, it was christened a "horseless carriage" (a brief description of how it works). "Cable television" accurately describes how that system works.

The biggest marketing successes come with basic, powerful explanations of the product being offered.

Years ago, a company called Tandem got a foothold in the market with "fault-tolerant" computers.

Prince revolutionized the tennis racquet business with "oversized racquets."

Orville Redenbacher shook up the popcorn market with "gourmet popping corn."

All these categories were quickly and easily understood. Customers knew what the companies were selling and how the products were really different.

Improving Your Category Name

There are times when you can adjust the explanation of what you're selling to improve your chances of success. A valve company called Keystone was selling what they called a "quarter-turn critical service valve." While this was an accurate description that reflected how the valve worked, it sure wasn't easy to figure out what they were selling. When I took a closer look inside the brochure that described this product, I discovered that this was simply a "zero leakage valve." That was a lot more exciting way to describe what they were selling.

A similar change in focus happened at General Mills during a discussion on how to increase the sales of their famous line of "Helpers" (hamburger, chicken, and tuna). They were traditionally sold as "extenders" that made meat go farther. This decidedly downmarket concept isn't a powerful idea in and of itself, especially when times are good.

Another way to look at this product is that all the different variations end up as a casserole of one sort or another. Because General

Mills sells hundreds of millions of dollars worth, you could also say that these Helpers are "America's favorite way to make a casserole." And they have 57 flavors and many Betty Crocker recipes to support this concept.

Appetizing casseroles cut across all income groups. (Hey, Martha Stewart makes them.) Even the American Institute of Cancer Research recommends them as a way to incorporate a wider variety of nutritious food into a single dish.

The key to making Hamburger Helper a bigger brand is coming up with a better expression of what they're selling.

Changing Can Be Tricky

You must adjust your category concept with care because it is difficult to change the minds of customers or prospects. With a modicum of experience in a product category, a consumer assumes that he or she is right. A mental perception is often interpreted as a universal truth. People are seldom, if ever, wrong—at least in their own minds.

Later chapters in this book provide examples of this problem, such as Xerox trying (without success) to convince people it is more than a copier company.

Why is Campbell's soup number one in the United States and nowhere in the United Kingdom? Why is Heinz soup number one in the United Kingdom and a failure in the United States? Marketing is a battle of perceptions, not products. Marketing is the process of dealing with those perceptions.

Once upon a time, some soft-drink executives believed that marketing is a battle of taste. The Coca-Cola Company produced a sweeter tasting cola and conducted 200,000 taste tests that proved "New Coke" tasted better than Pepsi-Cola and their original formula, now called "Coca-Cola Classic."

You know the end of the story. The soda that research showed tasted worst, Coca-Cola Classic, is today's best-selling cola. People weren't interested in New Coke.

You believe what you want to believe. You taste what you want to taste. Soft-drink marketing is a battle of perceptions, not of taste.

The "Truth Will Out" Mistake

The failure to understand the simple truth that marketing is a battle of perceptions trips up thousands of would-be entrepreneurs every year.

Marketing people are preoccupied with doing research and "getting the facts." They analyze the situation to make sure the truth is on their side. Then they sail confidently into the marketing arena, secure in the knowledge that they have the best product and that ultimately the best product will win.

It's an illusion. There is no objective reality. There are no facts. There are no best products. All that exists in the world of marketing are perceptions in the minds of customers or prospects. The perception is the reality. Everything else is an illusion.

Most marketing mistakes stem from the assumption that the marketer is fighting a product battle rooted in reality. What some marketing people see as the natural laws of marketing are based on a flawed premise that the product is the hero of the marketing program and that companies win or lose based on the merits of the product. Which is why the natural, logical way to market a product is invariably wrong.

The "Other Guy's Idea" Mistake

It's bad enough to launch a me-too product but equally problematic is a me-too idea: Two companies cannot own the same concept in the prospect's mind.

When a competitor owns a word or position in the prospect's mind, it is futile to attempt to own the same idea.

Volvo has preempted the concept of "safety." Many other automobile companies, including Mercedes-Benz and General Motors, have tried to run marketing campaigns based on safety. Yet no one except Volvo has succeeded in getting into the prospect's mind with a safety message.

Another massive marketing effort aimed at someone else's word can be found in bunny land—to be specific, the pink Energizer bunny that is trying to take the "long-lasting" concept away from Duracell. No matter how many bunnies Eveready throws into the fray, Duracell will still be able to hang onto the word *long-lasting*. Duracell got into the minds of customers first and preempted the concept. Even the "Dura" part of the name communicates it.

Researchers Can Mislead You

What often leads big companies down this booby-trapped lane is that wonderful stuff called research. Armies of researchers are employed, focus groups conducted, questionnaires tabulated—and what comes back in a three-pound report is a wish list of attributes that users want from a product or service. So if that's what people want, that's what we should give them.

What's the biggest problem people have with batteries? They go dead at the most inconvenient times. So what's the number one battery attribute? Long-lasting life, of course. If long-lasting is what people want, that's what we should advertise. Right? Wrong.

What researchers never tell you is that some other company already owns the idea. They would rather encourage clients to mount massive marketing programs. The theory is that if you spend enough money, you can own the idea. Right? Wrong.

Some years ago Burger King started down this slippery slope from which it has never quite recovered. A market study showed that the most popular attribute for fast food was "fast" (no big surprise there). So Burger King did what most red-blooded marketers do. It turned to its advertising agency and said, "If the world wants fast, our advertising should tell them we're fast."

What the research failed to underscore was that McDonald's was already perceived as being the fastest hamburger chain in the country. Fast belonged to McDonald's. Undaunted by this, Burger King launched its campaign with the slogan "Best food for fast times." The program quickly became a disaster. The advertising agency was fired, management was fired, the company was sold, and downward momentum was maintained (Chapter 8 focuses on Burger King).

Go "Opposite," Young Marketer

You can't own the same word or position that your competitor owns. You must find another word to own; you must seek out another attribute.

Too often a company attempts to emulate the leader. "They must know what works," goes the rationale, "so let's do something similar." Not good thinking.

It's much better to search for an opposite attribute that allows you to play off against the leader. The key word here is opposite—similar won't do.

Coca-Cola was the original and thus became the choice of older people. Pepsi successfully positioned itself as the choice of the younger generation. That was then. Recently, Pepsi was pushing "Joy," and Coke was pushing "Enjoy." Can you imagine, both pushing the same idea? Sounds like collusion to me.

Since Crest owned cavities, other toothpastes avoided cavities and jumped on attributes like taste, whitening, breath protection, baking soda, germ killing. You name it.

Marketing is a battle of ideas. So if you are to succeed, you must focus your efforts around an idea or attribute of your own. Without one, you had better have a low price. A very low price.

Marketers say all attributes are not created equal; some are more important to customers than others—you must try to own the most important attribute. All that is true but if the lead attribute is gone, you must settle for lesser business, which is far better than no business.

The "We're Very Successful" Mistake

Success often leads to arrogance and arrogance to failure. When people become successful, they tend to become less objective. They often substitute their own judgment for what the market wants.

As their successes mounted, companies like General Motors, Sears, and IBM became arrogant. They felt they could do anything they wanted in the marketplace. Success leads to trouble.

Digital Equipment Corporation brought us the minicomputer. Starting from scratch, DEC became an enormously successful $14 billion company. DEC founder Kenneth Olsen's success made Ken such a believer in his own view of the computer world that he pooh-poohed the personal computer, then open systems, and, finally, reduced instruction set computing (RISC). In other words, Ken Olsen ignored three of the biggest developments in the computer category. (A trend is like the tide—you don't fight it.) DEC's demise is dissected in Chapter 4.

The bigger the company, the more likely it is that the chief executive has lost touch with the front lines. This might be the single most important factor limiting the growth of a corporation. All other factors favor size. Marketing is war, and the first principle of warfare is force. The larger army, the larger company, has the advantage.

But the large company gives up some of that advantage if it cannot stay focused on the marketing battle that takes place in the mind of the customer.

The shootout at General Motors between Roger Smith and Ross Perot illustrates the point. When he was on the GM board, Ross Perot spent his weekends visiting dealers and buying cars. He was critical of Roger Smith for not doing the same.

"We've got to nuke the GM system," Perot said. He advocated atom-bombing the heated garages, chauffer-driven limos, and executive dining rooms. (Ross was a lot better at business than politics.)

Small companies are mentally closer to the front than big companies. That may be one reason for their rapid growth in the past decades. They haven't been tainted by success.

The "Everything for Everybody" Mistake

what is your product module?

When you try to be all things to all people, you inevitably wind up in trouble. Better advice comes from one manager who said, "I'd rather be strong somewhere than weak everywhere."

This kind of "all things" thinking leads to what is called "line extension."

In a narrow sense, line extension involves taking the brand name of a successful product (e.g., A.1. Steak Sauce) and putting it on a new product (e.g., A.1. Poultry Sauce).

not chicken

It sounds so logical. "We make A.1., a great sauce that gets the dominant share of the steak business. But people are switching from beef to chicken, so let's introduce a poultry product. And what better name to use than A.1. That way people will know the poultry sauce come from the makers of that great steak sauce, A.1."

But marketing is a battle of perception, not product. In the mind, A.1. is not the brand name, but the sauce itself. "Would you pass me the A.1. please?" asks the diner. Nobody replies: "A.1. what?"

Needless to say, the A.1. poultry launch was a dismal failure.

Blurring Your Difference

When you have a clear, well-expressed differentiating idea for your product, producing more versions only makes your message increasingly fuzzy.

Chevrolet was once a good value, a family car. It was number one in sales. Then endless versions made it a cheap, expensive, sedan, sports car, truck, van: Everything for everybody. Today it's number four in sales.

For many companies, line extension is the easy way out. Launching a new brand requires not only money but also an idea or concept. For a new brand to succeed, it ought to be first in a new category. Or the new brand ought to be positioned as an

some line ext are ok — others dilute brand

alternative to the leader. Big companies that wait until a new market has developed often find these two leadership positions already preempted. So they fall back on the old reliable line extension approach. Trouble usually ensues. (Chapter 10 spends more time on this mistake.)

The "Live by the Numbers" Mistake

Big companies are in a bind. On the one hand, Wall Street is staring at them asking, "How much are your sales and profits going to grow next month, next quarter, next year?" On the other hand, an endless number of competitors are staring at them saying, "We're not going to let you grow if we can help it."

So what happens? The CEO lies to Wall Street and then turns around to tell the marketing people what is expected in terms of profit and growth. They in turn scramble back to their offices and try to figure out how to make those unreasonable numbers.

Brash predictions about earnings growth often lead to missed targets, battered stock, and even creative accounting. But worse than that, they lead to bad decisions.

As panic sets in, upper management falls into the line extension, or the everything-for-everybody, trap to drive the numbers up. Rather than staying focused on being strong somewhere, they opt for being weak everywhere. Their only hope is that they will be promoted before it all hits the fan. As described in Chapter 2, that's exactly what happened at General Motors.

A Better Direction

Growth is the by-product of doing things right. But in itself, it is not a worthy goal. In fact, growth is the culprit behind impossible goals.

CEOs pursue growth to ensure their tenures and to increase their take-home pay. Wall Street brokers pursue growth to ensure their reputations and to increase their take-home pay.

A simpler and more powerful objective is to shoot for share, not profits. As a market emerges, your number one objective should be to establish a dominant market share. Too many companies want to take profits before they have consolidated their position.

What makes a company strong is not the product or the service. It's the position it owns in the mind. The strength of Hertz is in its leadership position, not the quality of its rent-a-car service. It's easier to stay on top than to get there.

Most financial moguls have a mathematical approach to marketing. The more businesses they're in, the faster they figure the business will grow. So, if you gather your courage and decide you will not let Wall Street run your business, what should you say to all those staring analysts?

You stand up and make what I call a "more is less" speech.

More Is Less

When you study categories over a long period, you can see that adding more can weaken growth, not help it. History has shown how difficult it is for big companies to hit a 15 percent target in earnings (a favorite number). But there remains no scarcity of executives willing to assume they can do it.

In its heyday (about 1980), Miller beer had two brands: High Life and Lite. Their sales ran about 35 million barrels of beer. Then they added Genuine Draft. By 1990, sales had slipped to 32 million barrels. Undaunted, they continued to add more and more Miller brands. Sales continued to go nowhere as Budweiser got stronger and stronger.

Finally, after almost 20 years of "more," their parent company, Philip Morris, came to town and fired the top management of Miller. (What took them so long?)

Philip Morris should know a "more is less" problem when they see one. The same thing happened to their flagship brand, Marlboro.

In an effort to maintain growth, Marlboro introduced Marlboro Lights into Marlboro Country. Then they introduced Marlboro

Mediums, then Marlboro Menthol, and even Marlboro Ultra-Lights. Suddenly, for the first time in memory, the brand started to turn down.

It's obvious what the problem was about: Real cowboys don't smoke menthols and ultra-lights.

Philip Morris isn't stupid. They are back in Marlboro Country with the red-and-white package. There's not a menthol or medium in sight in their advertising.

The Basic Problem

The more you add, the more you risk undermining your basic differentiating idea, which is the essence of your brand. If, as in Marlboro's case, the product stands for full flavor, how can that attribute hold up when the company starts to offer other flavors or weakened flavors?

Michelob was once a very successful, expensive full-flavored beer. Then it introduced Michelob Light and Michelob Dry. The brand went downhill. Heineken, another expensive full-flavored beer, obviously learned from that mistake. Their light beer was called Amstel Light, which is doing very nicely with the brilliant differentiating idea: "95 calories never tasted so imported."

Once upon a time, a company called Eveready had a strategy to offer whatever kind of battery you wanted. Then along came Duracell. They sacrificed a lot of business and offered only alkaline batteries.

Duracell became the specialist in long-lasting alkaline batteries and a differentiated success. But they were not the leader and had nothing to lose. The need for growth tends to make market leaders vulnerable. Rather than give up anything, they keep adding more. Most failed brands once had a good idea that they undermined by adding more and more versions.

Will this speech keep Wall Street at bay? Probably not, but it will make for one interesting analyst meeting.

The "Not Attacking Yourself" Mistake

Much has been written about the likes of DEC, Xerox, AT&T, and Kodak and their efforts to move from slow-growth to high-growth businesses. When this is exacerbated, companies are faced with what have been called disruptive technologies: DEC faced the desktop computer revolution; Xerox, the surge in laser printing; and Kodak, the digital camera.

Transforming a company when the underlying technology changes is no easy task. First of all, Wall Street is upset because lots of shareholder money starts to disappear in efforts that earn very little in return.

Traditional customers are often alienated as the sales force's attention becomes diffused by new ventures. The internal folks become very uncomfortable with all this change in the air.

Though difficult, leaders have no choice in this matter. They must find a way to move to that better idea or technology, even if it threatens their base business. If they don't, their future will be in question, especially as that technology is improved and picks up momentum.

It's a Question of "How"

The trick is to figure out how to shift horses. When Lotus found its 1-2-3 spreadsheet under attack as the PC world shifted to the Windows operating system and Microsoft's Excel for Windows had a running start, they made the right decision to put all their resources behind their Notes groupware product and all but give up their once dominant spreadsheet business. The story had a happy ending with IBM purchasing Lotus and Notes for $3.5 billion.

Gillette attacks its existing brands with new and improved blades. In essence, it's how they maintain a 60 percent share of the business. When they have a better blade, they use it against themselves.

One question is whether to launch a new brand or even a new company to better exploit what's happening in the marketplace. Cadillac should have quickly launched a new brand to counter the superpremium German and Japanese automobiles. They tried to use their Cadillac brand with no success (no "prestige" was the problem) and missed a very important segment in the market.

McDonald's tried to counter the rising success of pizza with McPizza, a dismal flop. Now they've bought a pizza chain called Donato's. A different brand is a better strategy.

It's a rapidly changing world out there. Not coping with change head-on probably causes more trouble than any other mistake.

The "Not Being in Charge" Mistake

When the CEO or high-level management doesn't take charge of strategy, things rarely go well. In today's rough-and-tumble world, marketing strategy is too critical to be left to middle-level management. After I make that "you're in charge" speech to general managers or CEOs, they often tell me that they don't want to undermine their employees. They want to give them the responsibility they were promised.

That's all well and good for morale, but I encourage them to think the Navy way.

When a naval vessel has a problem, the ultimate responsibility is not that of the young officer who had the conn when the accident occurred. It's the captain of the ship who must answer to that board of inquiry. And chances are, his career is in trouble.

In today's world, it's the CEO who has to answer to the board when things go bad. And as described in later chapters, a growing number are being asked to walk the plank.

These days it's your job on the line if you're at the top, so you'd better take charge.

2

General Motors

Forgetting What Made Them Successful

In the beginning, General Motors was a mess. Founded by William Durant in 1904, GM's core concept was to acquire a number of car companies at a time when this emerging industry was overrun with manufacturers. He figured when one was down another could be up and also that combining manufacture could save a lot of money. By 1910, he had acquired 17 car companies including Oldsmobile, Buick, and Cadillac.

In 1911, he invested in Louis Chevrolet who was designing what was called the Classic Six. By 1918, he owned Chevrolet, which was to replace Ford as the number one brand in the United States.

Enter Alfred Sloan

The year 1918 also was when Alfred Sloan came into the GM picture as Operating Vice President. He was associated with Pierre S. du Pont, who had invested heavily in GM stock. What Sloan inherited was what he called an "irrational product line" that had no guiding policy for its many brands of cars. The company's only objective was to sell the cars, which often took volume from each other. This is apparent when you look at the 1921 lineup and their prices:

Chevrolet	$ 795–$2,075
Oakland	$1,395–$2,065
Oldsmobile	$1,445–$3,300
Scripps Booth	$1,545–$2,295
Sheridan	$1,685
Buick	$1,795–$3,295
Cadillac	$3,790–$5,690

To make matters worse, all the cars in the line with the exception of Buick and Cadillac were losing money.

Sloan's first conclusion was that there were too many models and too much duplication. What they needed was a product policy (today, called a "multibrand strategy"). He set the number of models at five and separated them by price grades. It worked out to the following lineup:

Chevrolet	$ 450–$ 600
Pontiac	$ 600–$ 900
Buick	$ 900–$1,700
Oldsmobile	$1,700–$2,500
Cadillac	$2,500–$3,500

The basic policy was to mass-produce a full line of different cars that were graded upward in quality and price. The concept was to get people into the GM family and move them up. It was one of the earliest examples of market segmentation.

Honing the Brands

Under Sloan's guidance, GM honed its brands. He stressed the importance of marketing and brand image. He defined the division according to markets served and gave executives in each division their own initiative to compete for business.

Five distinct but strong brands emerged: Chevrolet, Pontiac, Buick, Oldsmobile, and Cadillac. These five brands moved General Motors to a point where they enjoyed over 57 percent of the U.S. car business. By the mid-1950s, pursuing more market share would only have attracted the feds and cries of "Break them up." This difficulty led to a terrible shift in strategy that started driving their market share downhill.

Make More Money

Because of their market dominance, the game shifted from making more and better cars to making more and more money from a relatively stable number of sales. In 1958, Frederic G. Donner, a finance man, became both chairman and CEO. Making cars was nice but making money became more important. Divisions were stripped of their autonomy.

I once had lunch with Frederic Donner. I was interested in his view on cars. What I got was a monologue on GM's organization and the difficulty of working with a large board of directors. He sure didn't think like Alfred P. Sloan. As Sloan's tenure in leadership receded, the "bean counters," as they were called, gradually took charge. Subtle changes in reporting and authorizations solidified the financial side's control.

Nothing dramatized this new direction more than the concept of "badge engineering." This invention of the finance staff was a way to increase profits "through uniformity." We can hear them now, "Hey, they're all cars. Why not interchange the parts?" Slowly but surely, the different brands lost their individuality both inside and outside the vehicle. It got so bad that *Fortune* did a cover story on the GM look-alikes: Chevrolet, Oldsmobile, Buick, and Pontiac. The article ran on August 22, 1983, and showed a photograph of these four models, side by side, in a field. They were all but identical. The article's title was prophetic: "Will Success Spoil General Motors?"

That uniformity made some money but undermined the brands' differences that Alfred had so painstakingly established. General Motors moved from a multiple-brand strategy to a similar-brand strategy.

Enter Roger Smith

The bean counters' high-water mark came when Roger Smith, a financial man, became chairman in 1981. The first thing he did was sell the GM building in New York and move much of the financial operation to Detroit. Under Smith's leadership, a significant number of financial men were appointed to the unlikely position of head of operating divisions.

It's not surprising that Smith lost sight of GM's most important audience, its customers. All this was brilliantly pointed on in Albert Lee's popular book, *Call Me Roger* (Velma Clinton, Chicago, 1988):

> By downplaying the psychological side of America's love affair with cars, he has placed GM years behind in styling, which sells.
>
> Roger, the accountant, who had never once been a plant manager or overseen the development of a single product of any kind, concluded that GM's answer to world competition would be robotics.

Nothing points to this strategy better than the *Fortune* (August 22, 1983) article mentioned earlier, which described a new assembly plant in Michigan:

> A surviving exemplar is the huge new assembly plant at Orion Township, Michigan, where GMAD will assemble 1984-model C cars, front-wheel drive big sedans. The $600-million plant bristles with robots, computer terminals, and automated welding equipment, including two massive $1.5-million Pbogate systems that align

and weld assemblies of body panels. Unmanned forklifts, guided by wires buried in the floor, will carry parts directly from loading docks. In its flexibility, Orion sets new standards for GM plants.

Regrettably, a lot of this fancy technology didn't work very well.

Back to 1921

The bean-counter legacy can best be dramatized by what happened to the plan of Alfred Sloan. When your focus is on making more money, your divisional managers very quickly learn on which side their bread is buttered. So to improve their numbers (and bonus), each GM division went beyond the parameters of the carefully constructed product policy that had been laid out. Chevrolet went up in price with fancier models, as did Pontiac. Buick and Oldsmobile went down in price for cheaper versions. When the dust settled, there were cars that not only looked alike but were priced alike. Take a look at the recent prices:

Saturn	$10,570–$21,360
Chevrolet	$13,995–$45,705
Pontiac	$16,295–$32,415
Oldsmobile	$18,620–$35,314
Buick	$26,095–$37,490
Cadillac	$31,305–$48,045

Recognize what has happened? It is 1921 all over again with poorly differentiated cars that compete with each other. Things are once again a mess. Their market share has declined from 57 percent of the U.S. business to 28 percent. For those of you who are interested in what that means in terms of money, it comes out to about $90 billion in lost sales. Losing sales like this leaves you with chronic excess capacity, no growth, and sticky labor issues.

Enter the Board

With the declining market share, it's not surprising that some years ago the board revolted and ejected top management. In recent years, we've seen new CEOs that weren't bean counters, a new marketing chief, brand managers: You name it and it's been tried. But nothing so far has seemed to drive that market share uphill.

The latest effort is the youngest CEO ever appointed. At 47, Rick Wagoner plans to dislodge the insular management style and to bring GM up to Internet speed with e-everything. Will this "Digital Drive" be enough? Will people want to buy GM cars because they are rolling communications devices that are connected to the Internet? Or because they have an "On Star" button on the dashboard? (Hey, Batman has one on his Bat Car.) Will a digital supply chain help GM make cars faster, cheaper, and more customized? Maybe it will. But GM's last fling with technology à la robotics didn't change things very much. And this brave new digital technology doesn't address the basic problem.

General Motors has forgotten what made them successful. It all comes down to the same situation that Sloan faced over 80 years ago. How could GM sort out and position their several brands so they would be different and work together on a complementary basis? The answer took major surgery in 1921 as Sloan exited two brands, consolidated activities, and repositioned what was left. Fixing things in 2001 will probably take major surgery again. Phasing Oldsmobile out is a good start but it won't be easy dealing with old customers, union complaints, and dealer problems.

At the same time, GM seems to be going in the opposite direction as it plans to lure younger buyers by rolling out seven new vehicles costing roughly $20,000 or less. Some will be redesigns of the slumping Saturn S-series and the Chevrolet Cavalier. And Chevy will pump up its low-end S-10 pickup into a mid-size. Pontiac will introduce the Vibe, a small sport wagon. You get the idea—adding more complexity to their already complex lineup of too many similar cars. By dropping one and adding seven, the confusion will continue, which is never good for business.

But that's their ongoing problem. Meanwhile, what can we all learn from General Motors' troubles?

 Beware of success.

Success often leads to arrogance and arrogance to failure.

Ego is the enemy of successful marketing. Objectivity is what's needed.

People who become successful tend to become less objective and often substitute their own judgment for what the market wants.

Success is often the fatal element behind the rash of line extensions. When a brand is successful, the company assumes the name is the primary reason for the brand's success. So they promptly look for other products to plaster the name on.

Actually the opposite is true. The name didn't make the brand famous (although a bad name might keep the brand from becoming famous). The brand got famous because the company made the right marketing moves. The steps they took were in tune with the fundamental laws of marketing.

They got into the mind first. They narrowed the focus. They preempted a powerful attribute.

The more you identify with your brand or corporate name, the more likely you are to fall into the line-extension trap. "It can't be the name," you might be thinking when things go wrong. "We have a great name." Pride goeth before destruction and a haughty spirit before a fall (Proverbs 16:18).

Actually, ego can be an effective driving force in building a business. What hurts is injecting your ego into the marketing process. Brilliant marketers have the ability to think the way a prospect thinks. They put themselves in the shoes of their customers. They don't impose their own view of the world on the situation. Keep in mind that the world is all perception anyway, and the only thing that counts in marketing is the customer's perception.

As General Motors' success mounted, the upper-level managers felt they could do whatever they wanted in the marketplace. Success leads to failure. The bean counters felt that they could do anything they wanted to make the cars more profitable. People would continue to buy them. Wrong.

Chevrolet was a hugely successful economical family car. That's why they figured they could line-extend it to become an expensive, sports car, truck, everything car. Wrong. That's why Chevrolet is no longer "the heartbeat of America" and is fourth in popularity. Toyota is number one.

Buick and Oldsmobile were very successful up-market cars. That's why management figured people would love cheaper versions. In this, they were right, but they didn't figure that lower prices would undermine the prestige of owning one of these brands.

Doing what you want to do because you're successful does not guarantee more success. You could achieve just the opposite—a guarantee of failure.

 Leaders have to block.

Strong competitive moves should never be ignored. Most companies have only one chance to win, but leaders have two. First, there is the initial win in becoming the leader. Then there is a win in copying a competitive move. But the leader must move rapidly before the attacker gets established.

Many leaders refuse to knock off their competition because their egos get in the way. Even worse, they bad-mouth the competitor's development until it's too late to save the situation.

Blocking works well for a leader because of the battleground. Remember, the war takes place inside the mind of the prospect. It takes time for an attacker to make an impression in the mind. Usually, there's time enough for the leader to cover.

For years, the U.S. automobile industry illustrated this principle well. Says John DeLorean in the book *On a Clear Day You Can See General Motors* (J. Patrick Wright, Wonder Book, 1979):

> Even though Ford was superior to General Motors in product innovation during the time I was with GM and Chrysler surpassed it in technical innovation, neither firm made substantial cuts into GM's half of the market.
>
> GM had not produced a significant, major automobile innovation since the hydromatic automatic transmission (1939) and the hard-top body style (1949). Ford pioneered in practically every major new market while Chrysler produced the significant technical innovations, such as power steering, power brakes, electric windows and the alternator.

But who gets credit for engineering excellence? General Motors, of course.

It's the flip side of the "truth will out" fallacy. The prospect also assumes that truth will out. Therefore, the prospect reasons that the market leader must have truth on its side; that is, the GM product is superior.

But this only works when you have those strong leadership perceptions going for you. This is no longer the case for GM. Its leadership perceptions took a fatal blow when they failed to block the small car when it came to the United States. And their quality standards didn't measure up to those of the Germans and Japanese.

Should a leader cover all bets or just the ones that are most likely to succeed? Although there's no point in covering downright silly ideas, who's to judge? When the first Volkswagen Beetle arrived, it looked strange indeed. "The three most overrated things in America," went a typical Detroit joke, "are Southern cooking, home sex, and foreign cars."

Many companies have lived to regret instant put-downs like this. Today, the watchword is more likely to be: "Let's monitor the situation and see what happens."

But that can be a dangerous tactic for a leader. Too often what happens, happens too fast. All of a sudden, it's too late to get into the new ball game. The Japanese quickly followed the Germans and before General Motors knew what hit them, the small car represented about 20 percent of the market and GM was outside looking in.

Ironically, the same thing happened at the upper end of the market: Mercedes and BMW started selling more expensive cars than Cadillac. GM failed to counter with a new brand in this category. (They should have brought back the LaSalle, a famous old expensive automobile.) Then the Japanese arrived with the Acura, Lexis, and Infinity.

Today a big part of the luxury market belongs to the Germans and Japanese. GM is on the outside looking in.

 **Don't lose touch.**

The bigger the company, the more likely it is that the chief executive has lost touch with the front lines. If you're a busy CEO, how do you gather objective information on what is really happening? How do you get around the propensity of middle management to tell you what they think you want to hear? How do you get the bad news as well as the good?

One possibility is to go "in disguise" or unannounced. This is especially useful at the distributor or retailer level. In many ways, this is analogous to the king who dresses up as a commoner and mingles with his subjects to get honest opinions about what's happening. Like kings, chief executives rarely get honest opinions from their ministers. There's too much intrigue going on at the court. So you must find an honest and trustworthy soul or two who can keep you informed on the bad news as well as the good. They could be lower level employees, or dealers, or customers. Someone that can tell you the unvarnished truth.

Consider the GM debacles with the small Cadillac (Cimarron and now Catera). Someone down in the trenches probably could have advised the CEO that Cadillacs that look like Chevrolets would never sell very well. And they didn't.

Another aspect of the problem is the CEO's allocation of time. There are too many United Way meetings, too many industry activities, too many outside board meetings, too many testimonial dinners. Strategy is too important to be turned over to an underling. If you delegate anything, you should delegate the chairmanship of the next fund-raising drive. (The vice president of the United States, not the president, attends state funerals.) In-house meetings are the next thing to cut back on. Instead of talking things over, walk out and see for yourself.

CHAPTER 3

Xerox

Predicting a Future That Never Came

M aking a clear, durable copy of anything was impossible in the B.C. age ("Before Carlson"). One had to use a thermography process that produced copies on an onionskin paper; they weren't very legible and began to fade not too long after they were filed.

Chester Carlson changed all this with the invention of plain paper copying, a system that used static electricity to transfer images from one piece of paper to another. He called this system xerography, a word derived from the Greek words for "dry" and "writing."

This wasn't an easy invention to sell. For 10 years, he wandered from company to company trying to find a buyer for his discovery. Finally a small New York-based photocopier paper company called Haloid acquired the right to develop a xerographic machine. Haloid changed its name to Haloid Xerox and, in 1959, introduced the Xerox 914, the first automatic copier (it made 7.5 copies per minute). *Fortune* called this big 650-pound copier, "the most successful product ever marketed in America." The rest is history. By 1968, company sales went over $1 billion, and it is now one of the 100 largest corporations in the United States.

A Fateful Prediction

On June 13, 1970, C. Peter McColough stood up at a shareholder's meeting and told of his plans to make Xerox a leader in information systems. Here was his rationale:

> Xerox and IBM are the two big companies exclusively in the information business. IBM owns the manipulative data processing part, and we own a part that puts things on paper. But the lines of separation are getting blurred, and it will be harder and harder to distinguish them. Sometime in the 1970s, we intend to be able to say to any big customer, "We can handle all your information needs." That includes data processing.

What Mr. McColough foresaw was the evolution of the business office, with the merging of communications, input, and output functions in an office automation system (now called "convergence"). That's why the company plunked down a billion dollars of Xerox stock to buy a computer company called Scientific Data Systems. They opened the Palo Alto Research Center (PARC), which produced some brilliant computer research (like the mouse) that made others rich and successful. They continued to pour money and more money into Xerox machines that couldn't make copies.

If You Fail, Try, Try Again

It didn't take long for that billion-dollar computer investment to fail. On July 21, 1975, Xerox Data Systems was killed in action and dutifully buried to the tune of an $85 million loss. But the loss of XDS didn't stop Xerox from trying.

In 1979, Xerox tried to get the facsimile business off the ground with the Telecopier line of products, with only modest success. "Funny, you don't look like a Xerox machine," said a typical ad. (This is what is called advertising the problem.) All this did was indicate the difficulty of differentiating Xerox from its copier position.

Another advertisement that illustrates the problem was the headline "How to tell the real Xerox from a Xerox copy." And again, they broadened the company's product line beyond copiers. They forgot the words of George Santayana: "Those who cannot remember the past are condemned to repeat it."

A review of Xerox's advertising and marketing of the 1980s shows that effort was not lacking. Although a multipage ad showed a broad range of different products, it left readers with the impression that Xerox was a copier company that happened to make a lot of other equipment that wasn't selling very well.

Even an advertisement specifically for Xerox Computer Services needed seven warnings to tell the reader, "This is not about copiers." No matter what Xerox tried to sell, it couldn't seem to get away from its copier position.

In November 1978, Xerox announced the XTEN network. *Business Week* reported the event in its November 27, 1978, issue:

> If all goes according to plan, Xerox says it will be operating the network in selected cities by 1981, eventually spreading to 200 metropolitan areas. This timetable would put Xerox head to head with IBM's Satellite Business network. Despite the risks involved, the move into network services could be critical for Xerox if it is to maintain itself as a major supplier of the office of the future.

For all the planning, the XTEN network didn't make it. But this failure didn't deter Xerox.

In December 1979, the Ethernet office network was launched with high hopes that were quickly dashed.

A year and a half later, the 8010 Star workstation was launched. This was followed shortly thereafter by the 820 information processor, or personal computer as the industry preferred to call it.

"Xerox's Bid to Be No. 1 in Offices" said the headline of an article in the June 22, 1981, issue of *Business Week*. "Now the industry will know our secret for certain," declared W. Dal Berry, vice-president and general manager of Xerox's Office Products business unit. "And that is, we want to be No. 1 in this market."

"We think the 820 could accelerate the move to office automation," declared Berry with some bravado. "We're not selling the future—the future is now."

The year 1984 marked a change in Xerox strategy. No longer would copier sales reps sit on the sidelines. Xerox threw the entire team into the office automation battle. Team Xerox was the code name for this project launched with high hopes.

They ran advertisements that showed the team with the full line of products they were assigned to sell. "We'd suggest talking to a company that offers more than just typewriters. Or just copiers. Or just computers," said the advertisement. "In other words, talk with a company that makes a whole line of office products." Of course, it did make sense to talk with such a company. Unfortunately, most people were going to IBM to talk.

The full-line approach was represented by a Xerox ad that asked, "Which type of printer should you buy?" The ad went on to suggest five different printers. Meanwhile, IBM doubled the bet and raised Xerox two by running an advertisement that offered 12 different printers.

It was at this point that the following lesson became painfully obvious.

 **If you're known for one thing, the market will not give you another thing.**

Despite Xerox's enormous effort, history taught this company:

- Xerox can't reach beyond copiers with computers.
- Xerox can't reach beyond copiers with Ethernet.
- Xerox can't reach beyond copiers with Team Xerox.

People will give you what made you famous, no more. And if Xerox had looked into the minds of its prospects, it would have quickly seen that moving into office information systems was never in the cards.

In the midst of all this effort, the trade publication *Information Week* conducted a survey of a sample of its subscribers that was summarized in this report: "Office Information Systems in the Large Corporate Environment." (*Information Week* had 100,000 subscribers, 80 percent of which represented companies with 1,000 or more employees. It would seem that this was the heart of the office automation market.)

When these subscribers were asked, "Which manufacturers of office information systems are you most interested in?" IBM scored a whopping 81 percent. After all that effort, Xerox didn't even make the charts. In the minds of even the most sophisticated business executives, any Xerox machine that didn't make a copy just didn't compute.

What Should Xerox Have Done?

Xerox management actually asked me this question in 1985. My basic message to Xerox was to stop fighting copiers. You can't change what's in the prospect's mind. I suggested they should start using copiers—their strongest asset in a strategic war with IBM and AT&T.

This was summed up as "the third leg strategy." It was a way for Xerox to take advantage of its heritage. As with many strategies, it's helpful to step back and get a sense of what has been going on in the marketplace. I refer to this as "studying the context of the category."

The office of the past had three legs: To put yourself in business, you got a telephone from AT&T (the communications leg), a typewriter from IBM (the input leg), and a copier from Xerox (the output leg).

When you look at the office of the present, the action has been in the input leg. The typewriter was supplanted by the word processor, which is being supplanted by the computer. The telephone and copier legs have scarcely changed at all.

What about the office of the future, a concept on which Xerox bet so heavily? If you believe everything you read, the office of the future will have a single leg that comprises the office automation system. It will be supplied primarily by a single vendor, and in 1985 IBM was everyone's bet. But the office of the future is still out there in the future for the simple reason that single-vendor systems don't always sell.

A high-fidelity audio system was never marketed profitably by one vendor because consumers picked the receivers and the disk and tape players they wanted. The same went for the home entertainment center and GE's dream of selling all the major appliances in the kitchen. Buyers preferred to pick their own favorite brands. General Electric couldn't even sell a turnkey electric power plant as utilities assembled their components of choice.

Why don't one-stop systems sell? Here are some reasons: It's too big a decision; companies would rather buy one piece at a time. It's too big a purchase; companies are not used to buying offices the way they buy plants. It's too big a commitment; nobody wants to be locked into a long-term relationship with a single supplier.

A Third Leg Scenario

Instead of suggesting the impossible, the third leg scenario offers a view of an office of the future that still has three legs. The AT&T

communications leg will add voice mail and facsimile. The IBM input or processing leg will add workstations, servers, and networks. The question is what will Xerox add to the output or printing leg? The merging of legs is an unlikely prospect because history points to the difficulty of "cross-leg" activities.

There are, however, output opportunities for Xerox as companies add computer printers, scanners, and storage devices to the output side of the office.

In 1985, the three basic recommendations to Xerox were:

1. Start with what Xerox owns in the mind of the prospect.
2. Sell the hottest new technology in the office field today.
3. Preempt the new technology in the same way Xerox did once before.

The hottest new technology in the office then was the laser, the "super tool of the 1980s." Everywhere people turned, the laser was making a dramatic appearance. GTE was bouncing laser beams off the moon. In communications, the laser was beginning to replace satellites. There was laser surgery, laser videodisks, laser-welding systems, laser star war satellites, laser typesetting and, most importantly, laser printers.

These machines were beginning to explode in the office. In June 1984, Hewlett-Packard introduced the Laser Jet at $3,500. They sold 10,000 units in three months. Datek was predicting that the market in 1985 would reach 100,000 units. This was the future that was about to come. How could Xerox preempt it?

Preempting the Laser

In the past 30 years, three technologies have roared through the office and into our language:

1. *Thermography* by 3M, a photocopying process that used infrared rays to product a copy on a special type of paper.

2. *Xerography* by Xerox, a copying process that used the action of light to produce a copy on plain paper.

3. The *microprocessor* technology that IBM has dominated.

I saw an opportunity for Xerox to put another technological word in a yet-to-be-published edition of the dictionary: *lasography*.

To me, lasography said a lot. It was new and different, and the business world loves things that are new and different. It sounds like a basic technology somehow related to xerography. In other words, it connects to Xerox's last big technology. It is from Xerox, the only company that's perceived to be in the "ography" business. It uses lasers, which are perceived to be on the leading edge of technology.

And Xerox had the perfect credentials to preempt this technology: In 1977, the Xerox 9700 electronic printing system was the first xerographic laser printer. They were in a perfect position to do what IBM did in PCs by coming in after the fact and taking over the market. Consider the IBM microscenario:

- IBM develops large computers.
- Apple, Radio Shack, and others introduce small computers.
- The market takes off.
- IBM introduces the PC and takes over the market.
- IBM uses the PC to sell office networks.

Now consider what could have been the Xerox scenario:

- Xerox develops large printers.
- Hewlett-Packard and Corona introduce small printers.
- The market starts to take off.
- Xerox introduces the small laser printer and takes over the market.
- Xerox uses the laser printer to sell networks and other products.

Then why did Xerox let Hewlett-Packard run off with this multi-billion-dollar market unchallenged? Well, that leads to yet another faulty prediction about the future.

Ion Deposition?

After I set forth the recommended strategy to the then CEO, he asked me to go out to the West Coast where I presented it to the group in charge of all noncopier information system products.

There I was, facing a room full of technical and marketing people who were dutifully executing the office automation strategy that had been in force for years. I was the designated outside messenger bringing the bad news that all their past efforts were in vain and they should focus on the lowly laser printer instead of their glorious office machines. This was not a popular message.

To this day, 15 years later, I have a vivid memory of an interchange that ended the meeting. After listening to my impassioned plea about laser printing, an engineer in the back of the room stood up and said that laser printing was "old hat." Xerox had seen the future and it was about to be "ion deposition." I asked what that was. The reply was that it was a little hard to explain to a layperson, but it was going to be fast and cheap. My response went something like this, "When that happens, we can move to ionography, but for now let's jump on the laser and lasography." The room went icy cold, the sale was lost, and another prediction was pursued that never happened.

Big Trouble at Xerox

Today, Xerox is surrounded by alligators. The decisions made after that ill-fated meeting cost them billions. Although, they finally jettisoned all those noncopier products and are focused on being a "document company," they lost focus on their base business, thus allowing competition to take away their most important customers.

Heidelberger Druckmaschinen A.G. of Germany, Canon Inc. of Japan, and most recently IBM (with a high-speed copier using the Heidelberger engine) are making deep inroads into the extremely high-speed copiers that are Xerox's most profitable product line. Canon and Ricoh are cutting heavily into the next-fastest machines. And Hewlett-Packard, the main rival in printers, is riding along relatively untouched. And what I once predicted has happened. Copies made on laser and inkjet printers now exceed copies made on copiers. It's no wonder Xerox's numbers have gotten so bad. Ironically, by misreading the future, Xerox surrendered its future to Hewlett-Packard and Japanese copier rivals.

Heads are rolling, the stock has plummeted, and there's even talk of being acquired. And the *Wall Street Journal* reported that Xerox has urged its own employees to stop making, of all things, copiers, unless absolutely necessary. That's what I call big trouble.

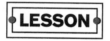 **You can't predict the future.**

I never cease to be amazed at how many people, like C. Peter McColough, boldly step forward and make those brave predictions. But when you look back on them you quickly discover how wrong even the futurists are. Consider the following:

- An analysis was made of predictions from Herman Kahn, director of the Hudson Institute think tank, in the 1960s and 1970s. The predictions were 75 percent wrong.
- Futurist John Naisbitt's popular 1982 book *Megatrends 2000* identified 10 trends that would shape our future. An analysis of those predictions showed that three megatrends were already well established before 1982. Seven trends never materialized.

Well, you could argue, they have to go out on a limb because it's their job. Fair enough, so let's look at business press forecasts. An analysis was made of technology predictions published between

1958 and 1989 in such places as the *Wall Street Journal*, the *New York Times*, *Business Week*, *Fortune*, and *Forbes*.

They were 80 percent wrong.

Trying to predict what the office of the future would be like and then betting Xerox on that prediction was a long-shot gamble that came up snake eyes.

A variation on the difficulty of predicting the future is trying to research the future. Not many years ago, fax machines were found in only a few large offices. Today, they are ubiquitous and are rapidly spilling out of the office and into the home. The fax machine is American in invention, technology, design, and development. And U.S. manufacturers, such as Xerox, had fax machines they could have taken to market. Yet not one fax machine being sold in the United States today is American-made.

The Americans did not aggressively push fax machines on the market because market research convinced them that there was no demand for such a gadget. Despite the well-known fact that one cannot conduct market research on something not in the market, researchers went out and asked people: "Would you buy a telephone accessory that costs upward of $1,500 and enables you to send, for $1 a page, the same letter the post office delivers for 25 cents?" The answer, predictably, came back "no."

Finally, even some futurists are getting uncomfortable with the profession of prognostication. "Futurism isn't prediction anymore," says Douglas Rushkoff, author of the pop-culture chronicle *Cyberia* (HarperCollins, 1994). "It's state-of-the-art propaganda. It's future creation. Futurists put their clients in a state of fear and then explain that they hold the secret knowledge that can save them."

 **Never forget what made you famous.**

At the heart of Xerox's problem was a loss of focus on the essence of their business. Simply stated, it was "putting marks on paper." It was what made them famous, and it was at the heart of their technology. And it wasn't as if we were heading into a paper-less world. Today, despite all the digital talk about less paper, the average white-collar office worker uses over 250 pounds of copier paper a year.

What Xerox did at that first disastrous decision in 1970 was to see itself, along with IBM, as being in the "information business." Wrong.

It was wrong because the world saw Xerox copying information, not generating or communicating information. And a company's efforts have to line up with the way the world sees that firm.

Where Many Lose Focus

Most big companies head off in the wrong direction at a point that could aptly be described as "delusions of grandeur."

Upper management perceived Xerox to be a successful technology company. The world saw them as a copier company.

Successful companies are quick to go beyond what made them successful and assign grander attributes to themselves.

IBM was perceived as a major supplier of business machines but could they sell copiers? Nope. Nor could they sell telephone systems, which they tried. No more than AT&T, a widely respected communications company, could sell computers, although they blew several billion dollars trying.

What most miss is that in a competitive world, you have to stay focused on your specialty.

The Advantages of the Specialist

People are impressed with those who concentrate on a specific activity or product. They perceive them as experts and tend to attribute more knowledge and experience to these specialists than they sometimes deserve. This isn't surprising when you consider the definition of *expert:* "one having much training and knowledge in some special field."

Conversely, people rarely describe a generalist as having expertise in many fields of endeavor, no matter how good he or she may be. Common sense tells the prospect that a single person or company cannot be expert in everything.

Xerox was a specialist in copying, nothing else. Consumers would not grant them expertise in computers or other related equipment that did not put marks on paper. It was not a question of whether the company could do it. It was a question of the marketplace judging whether Xerox had the same expertise as the perceived specialists.

This is not to say that a company cannot broaden the perception of its expertise. Xerox certainly could talk about the many ways they can produce, store, and distribute documents electronically, which should be their focus.

That's their specialty and, if they had done things right, it would have been difficult for others to come in and take their business, especially since their major competitors are not perceived as specialists in putting marks on paper.

Once understood, all of Xerox's efforts in R&D, sales, and marketing would have gone into an effort to maintain their edge and leadership in the ability to put marks on paper. In that way, they wouldn't have squandered money, effort, and management on businesses they had no hope of winning. A company gets distracted, which only opens the doors to competitors.

Ironically, Xerox's R&D efforts were widely successful as they developed things like the mouse, Ethernet, graphical user interfaces, and flat-panel displays. Many of these developments shaped the computer revolution from which others reaped the benefits.

Because of their "marks on paper" perception, the only R&D development that Xerox could have truly exploited was the laser printer, which they invented at PARC. It became the backbone of the desktop publishing industry that Hewlett-Packard now dominates.

 Lack of leadership is often the problem.

Experience has shown that bad things happen when the CEO doesn't take an active role in developing strategy and keeping things focused. Good leaders know where a company should go and lead the charge. They have a deep understanding of what made the company successful, and they always keep that in focus.

When the then Xerox CEO sent me off to see what the troops thought about our laser focus strategy, I should have realized that whatever I said would not change their attitude. The only one who could have done that was the CEO himself.

After all, they must have thought, who is this stranger telling Xerox veterans that what we've been working on all these years is something we shouldn't be working on? And when did the corporate strategy change?

In the middle of companies, there often are people with a bad case of "personal agenda." They are trying very hard to put their mark on something so as to progress up the corporate ladder. They make their decisions based not only on what's good for the company but on what's good for their careers. Or worse, they are trying to avoid mistakes that could imperil their careers. They certainly aren't going to stand up and question a company's vision or tell the emperor that he has no clothes.

They were looking at a strategy for the company that essentially challenged their soon-to-be-announced effort to try to sell a new generation of computer systems. Why would any midlevel executive say, "That makes more sense than what I've been working on." The only question they could have asked was, "Why isn't the CEO here telling us to change direction?"

Ironically, the reason I got to present to the CEO was that the number two man at Xerox had listened to my recommendations and began to see the error of what they were trying to do. But even though this executive now realized it was the wrong decision, he couldn't openly admit to a mistake of that magnitude. Only the CEO was in a position to change the plans that had been approved and presented to the board several years earlier.

That's probably why the CEO sent me out as the messenger. He figured I would get shot and he wouldn't be embarrassed by having to undo a faulty decision.

He was right.

CHAPTER 4

Digital Equipment Corporation

From Number Two to Nowhere

One can accurately compare DEC to a shooting star. Back in 1957, when a computer was a room-sized monster that cost millions of dollars and needed a sterile, air-conditioned chamber, Ken Olsen set out to make a smaller, cheaper, and easier-to-use computer for the mass market. His company, Digital Equipment Corporation, gave birth to a revolution by developing the first mass-produced minicomputer.

By the 1970s, companies were distributing minicomputers throughout their operations rather than concentrating their data processing in one large mainframe machine. DEC rode the trend to become the second-largest computer maker in the world, after giant International Business Machines Corporation.

A Fateful Meeting

But the threat of a mass-produced desktop computer called a PC loomed on the horizon. Stan Olsen, Ken's younger brother and one of DEC's founders, saw the desktop as both a threat and as an opportunity. The threat was that IBM was working on a small computer that was soon to be introduced. The opportunity was that one of DEC's smaller minicomputers could be the heart of a more powerful desktop machine than that of IBM.

Stan didn't have much leverage with his older brother, so he hired me to help him sell his brother on the importance of developing a desktop computer to counter the IBM threat. He saw a natural selling platform:

> IBM got famous by selling big computers to business. DEC got famous by selling small computers to business. That's why it's more natural for DEC to introduce a small serious desktop machine for business.

A meeting was called in Ken Olsen's office to discuss the issue. It turned out to be a meeting that sealed DEC's fate.

"Beat Their Specs"

In a small conference room in Maynard, Massachusetts, I made the case for DEC's entry into the business and their superior credentials over the likes of Apple and other home PCs. We waited for Ken Olsen's response. After a short silence, Ken indicated he wasn't moved much by the presentation and his brother's entreaties.

I remember responding that the real problem was IBM and their launch of a PC. Because of IBM's strong business credentials, DEC would then have little opportunity to introduce a small serious business computer.

Ken stood up and made a speech I'll never forget. He said that he didn't want to be first. What he wanted to do is to see what they came up with and then "beat their specs." He took out an imaginary pair of six-shooters to dramatize DEC's ability to shoot holes in the faulty engineering behind IBM's PC.

What went through my mind was a picture of two German officers sitting high up on a Normandy cliff on D-Day. As far as the eye could see, there were landing ships and vessels of every kind. One officer said to the other, "What should we do?" His companion said, "Nothing. Let's see what they do and then we'll make our move."

The result would be the same. After the invasion, it was over.

A few years later, Ken relented and DEC introduced not one, but three PCs (the Professional 325 and 350, the Rainbow 100, and the DECmateII). The result was total confusion and few sales.

The Invasion Rolls On

DEC's traditional minicomputer business began to be whittled away by a growing number of competitors. Microcomputer companies— replacing the mini's chip-laden circuit boards with a simpler design using a microprocessor, or computer-on-a-chip—introduced compact units that did much of what DEC's more powerful machines could do, and sold for a fraction of their price.

DEC's delay in developing its own family of easy-to-use desktop and office computers gave the microcomputer makers a head start in attracting the horde of neophyte end-users who had little appreciation for DEC's technological expertise. But Ken Olsen still wasn't impressed. In the May 2, 1983, edition of *Business Week*, he was reported to have said: "The personal computer will fall flat on its face in business because users want to share files and want more than one user on the system," he asserted. "Under those circumstances, the minicomputer becomes more important than ever. Our strategy emphasizes the mini."

That was both a bad prediction and a losing strategy.

Restructuring after restructuring failed to turn things around. Less than 10 years later, Ken Olsen was forced out of the company he had founded. Losses mounted. Employees were fired and the stock plummeted. Finally Compaq bought the company, and for all practical purposes DEC is gone. It's ironic that they were taken over by a PC company. The development that Ken Olsen pooh-poohed turned into a monster that devoured him and his company.

What lessons are there in DEC's demise?

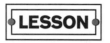 **Never underestimate a bigger competitor.**

Sometimes you can get away with ignoring smaller competitors. But you must take a big competitor's moves seriously, especially if they are far bigger than you. First and foremost, you must try to evaluate what will happen to you if they succeed. If their success could seriously impact your business, you have no other option but to strike first to blunt their move or preempt their strategy (the same goes for war).

A "Business" Computer

What DEC could have done was adopt brother Stan's strategy of introducing the first serious small computer for business by positioning their desktop line as an alternative to the personal computer. The business computer strategy they could have developed would have been expressed as follows:

> A personal computer is fine for your home. But for your business you need a business computer that is powerful, expandable, and compatible. And it's a computer from DEC, the second largest computer company in the world.

As this was all unfolding, it was shakeout time in the small computer field. The papers were filled with companies in trouble: Osborne, Fortune, Texas Instruments. The resulting fear and confusion in the market was playing into the hands of IBM. Credentials in the business sector were the most important sales tools and DEC had them if they chose to use them.

Of course, DEC would have had to embrace such things as open systems (Ken Olsen also didn't think much of this), other networking alternatives beyond their own, and a massive software development effort. But by focusing on small serious computers for business and selling office computer systems rather than IBM's office automation systems, they would have had a chance to become a strong alternative to IBM.

But that chance melted away as the desktop world roared on without DEC as a player.

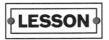 **When you've got a chance, try to become the next thing.**

Our story isn't quite over. In 1993, the same year that Ken Olsen retired, DEC introduced the Alpha AXP, the first advanced 64-bit architecture, into a 32-bit world.

And, since Ken was gone, I was asked back to DEC to discuss how this new development should be introduced against the backdrop of all DEC's current problems.

What I saw as possible was a last-ditch effort to turn things around in a way that was a repeat of their history. The cornerstone of their earlier success was the 1980 introduction of the first 32-bit VAX architecture into a 16-bit world. It turned out to be the "next thing" in the computer world.

Being the Latest

In this high-tech, rapidly changing world, people have become accustomed to the "next generation" of products. It's not only anticipated, but also expected.

Rather than try to be better, I advise companies to try to be next. That's a sure way to be different. The psychology is obvious. No one is comfortable buying what could be perceived as an obsolete product. So the way to leapfrog your competition is to position yourself as what's new and better, with emphasis on the new.

For years, I have preached that strong leaders attack themselves with next-generation products. No one has done this better than Intel. This march of microprocessors has been a marvel to behold: the 286, the 386, the 486, the Pentium, the Pentium II, the Pentium III, and the Pentium III Xeon. They have dominated the sophisticated chip business by constantly introducing the next generation at the expense of their existing microprocessors. That way, no competitor has been able to mount an attack, even on price. (Yes, that's a lower price, but it's a lower price on an obsolete chip.)

As mentioned, Gillette's strategy of introducing the next generation of razor blade is also an example of using this approach to dominate a market.

The same goes for GE's efforts to improve the humble lightbulb. Their latest offering is a bulb called Enrich. This unique blue glass bulb brings out the vibrant colors in furnishings and decoration by heightening color contrast.

Being the latest is at the heart of starting a new category.

The Law of the Category

In *The 22 Immutable Laws of Marketing* (HarperCollins, 1993), myself and Al Ries (my former partner) wrote that if you can't be first, set up a new category in which you can be first. IBM was first in computers, so DEC pioneered a new category in minicomputers. The trick is how to invoke this law. No one did it better than Advil when they ran an ad that published the generations of pain relief:

Bayer aspirin	1899
Tylenol acetaminophen	1955
Advil ibuprofen	Today

They didn't spend a lot of time talking about pain relief. And if you were to market-research ibuprofen, you would probably find people who know very little about it other than that it's "advanced medicine for pain."

Here's a fact of life. Prospects prefer ibuprofen to acetaminophen not because they know anything about the drug, but because ibuprofen has been positioned as the next generation.

That's what DEC had to do for its next generation 64-bit Alpha chip.

Using the Advil analogy, they should have reintroduced the desktop computer generations:

1. Apple pioneered the 8-bit home computer.
2. IBM pioneered the 16-bit office computer.
3. Sun pioneered the 32-bit UNIX workstation.

That set up the opportunity that was there for the taking: DEC could have pioneered the 64-bit workstation.

But the fact of life DEC had to live with was that prospects would prefer 64-bit workstations, not because they knew anything about those workstations, but because they were the next generation.

Their increased power wouldn't sell. The "next generation" would.

The Story That Was Never Told

I recommended that DEC seize the opportunity to launch the 64-bit generation of workstations. The credentials for this launch were that DEC pioneered the 32-bit VMS operating system and VAX architecture to become the world's second largest computer company.

The way to dramatize this was to simply replay history by reminding the marketplace, "They laughed when DEC introduced the 32-bit VAX minicomputer." To do this, they should republish the negative review. Here's the way I recommended the story could have been told:

> In 1979, DataQuest reported, "Digital's architectural change is highly questionable. Software developers and end-user customers currently have *no* need for the technological advances that Digital's new chip-set offers, nor will they in the foreseeable future."
>
> They obviously were very wrong.
>
> Two years ago, DEC introduced the 64-bit Alpha architecture. The experts once again yawned. While acknowledging its speed and power, insiders questioned as they did in 1979 whether it's needed.
>
> Will history repeat itself?

Sacrifice Was Called For

This strategy called for a major focus on alpha workstations, not the personal computers, minicomputers, and other services that DEC was also selling. They had to sacrifice the promotion of other products.

This approach was based on the knowledge that what you advertise, what you sell, and what you make money on can be three different things.

"What you advertise" is what we were focusing on. That's the part that builds perceptions in the mind. That's the part that gets you in the door and, in this case, could save DEC's reputation.

The story they had to tell to sell was that the 64-bit Alpha was the "next thing."

DEC might have been the world leader in small business computers. That was an opportunity missed. DEC might have been the world leader in 64-bit workstations. That also turned out to be an opportunity missed, which leads us to the next lesson learned the hard way.

 Perilous times require perilous action.

Steve Milunovich is one of Merrill Lynch's premier analysts. Some time after my proposal to DEC, he was visiting with Bob Palmer, the CEO who had replaced Ken Olsen.

Steve, who was aware of the proposal, asked Palmer why he did not focus on the 64-bit workstation market.

He had an interesting observation that said a lot about the problems a CEO faces when there is big trouble. His comment went something like: "I didn't want to get niched. We're more than just an alpha chip company."

What he failed to grasp was the simple concept of "better niched than dead." Without a winner, DEC could never turn around its declining perceptions. When *Business Week* writes an article about you that's headlined "Desperate Hours at DEC," you know that your customers and prospects are saying "Hello" to IBM or Sun or Hewlett-Packard. No one, especially any company buying high-technology computers, wants to be left with an orphan.

When a company's reputation is in the balance, a CEO's only choice is to go for whatever idea that has a chance to turn things around. DEC's minicomputer business was in decline. DEC's PC business was under cost pressures. All that was left was a bold move into the workstation business that was on the ascendancy. (Sun has done very well by it.)

One could say it was a perilous move. No doubt. And would it have worked? Who knows? But at that moment they had a shot. When the moment passed, they were in more than big trouble. They were toast.

The truth is that Bob Palmer had no other bet to make. As mentioned, Jim Manzi, the CEO of Lotus, had only one bet and it was Notes. He spent $500 million developing momentum for the product. He had to fight with his management and the board about it, but he hung in there. If he hadn't, that $3.5 billion offer would never have arrived from IBM. Lotus would have been run over by Microsoft.

As one military historian put it, "The true test of a general is not when he is advancing. The true test is when he has to retreat."

To that I say, "Amen."

CHAPTER 5

AT&T

From Monopoly to Mess

In 1875, Alexander Graham Bell received funding for his work on the "talking telegraph." He founded American Bell. Ten years later, American Telephone & Telegraph was incorporated as a wholly owned subsidiary of American Bell and began work on the first long-distance network. By the end of the century, local telephone use expanded dramatically, and AT&T acquired the assets of its parent company, American Bell. It then went on to build an amazing telephone company that was the envy of the world.

But, as the *Wall Street Journal* so neatly reported in September 2000, "After more than a century of binding America together with sound waves and wire, AT&T Corporation, once the country's biggest, wealthiest and strongest company, is itself unraveling."

What Went Wrong?

That same article went on to point out the reasons behind AT&T's 115-year rise and fall. The first was that no company, however large, is immune from economic and technological change. And communications certainly had changed dramatically from the Bell System's good old monopoly days of the 1950s and 1960s. But that's no excuse, a company must learn to cope with change.

The other reason given for the company's downward spiral was that AT&T lost touch with their customers when the government forced them to divest themselves of the Baby Bells in 1982. They no longer owned the "dial tone" and thus lost a great deal of their muscle while having to pay the "Babies" a piece of every long-distance call. Sure, they lost their local exchange business, but they still had their equipment, their long-distance, and their corporate business.

The unraveling actually lies in what they did and didn't do to themselves; it was more of a problem than what others did to them. They made those mistakes because "competition" was a new experience for a company that had always been a "natural monopoly." They had no sense of how tough it is in the real world where everyone is out to get your business.

The Computer Mistakes

When the Baby Bells went out on their own in 1984, it freed up AT&T to pursue other business outside its monopoly. Over the years, AT&T had acquired considerable technological finesse through its Bell Laboratories. They had developed specialized switches, the UNIX operating system, computer languages, and computers they used internally.

So someone made the naive decision to challenge IBM's dominance in corporate information technology. Conquering the computer industry seemed like the silver lining in the cloud that hung over AT&T when they had to give up their monopoly. The inexperienced AT&T marketers thought the transition into computers would be easy. (After all the highly publicized carnage suffered by others that took on IBM, one wonders what planet these folks inhabited.)

First up, the company formed a strategic alliance with Olivetti U.S.A. to develop and market PCs. (Can you imagine, an Italian computer company?) Out rolled the PC6300 and 3BZ, which was a line of minicomputers. People looked at these and asked one question: Where's the phone? Neither swept away corporate buyers.

Then in 1991, AT&T plopped down $7.3 billion for computer maker NCR. (Can you imagine, a cash register computer company?) Then they pumped in another $2.8 billion into the beleaguered business. NCR turned out to be another giant loser as the market shifted from mainframes to networks of smaller computers.

After a decade, AT&T junked the PCs and spun off the losing NCR. Both ventures cost the company billions as well as untold management energy. As Sheldon Hocheiser, AT&T's corporate historian (how many companies have one of these?) aptly commented, "It turns out that there is an enormous difference between having R&D experience in computing and having marketplace expertise."

Using some of that money to squeeze their new long-distance competitors, MCI and Sprint, would have made a lot more sense. Or they could have put it into building a next generation local network to compete with the Baby Bells. Either way it would have been money better spent.

The Cable Television Mistake

In 1997, C. Michael Armstrong rode in from IBM and Hughes Electronics Corporation to clean up the town. His opening statement in the 1998 Annual Report spelled trouble: "We're transforming AT&T from a long-distance company to an 'any-distance' company. From a company that handles mostly voice calls to a company that connects you to information in any form that is useful to you—voice, data and video. From a primarily domestic company to a truly global company."

Recognize that? It's the everything-for-everybody mistake. That speech might have played back in their monopoly days, but when he gave it, the company was surrounded by well-positioned competitors specializing in one thing or another. It was almost a replay of the speech that the Xerox CEO gave about getting into computers.

But off they went. Armstrong decided to get back that local business through cable. He plopped down $115 billion for TCI and the Media One Group cable systems although many felt they were over-priced. Despite all this money, AT&T still had only what some described as a Swiss-cheese footprint over the United States that left many large unserved holes.

Then the fun began as billions had to be invested to upgrade these video lines to accommodate voice. Armstrong underestimated the complexity of all this as well as the fundamental problem of getting a consumer to switch to cable telephony—sign-up numbers fell well below their estimates. A cartoon that captured the difficulty of all this showed man with a large Sony TV on his shoulder saying into it, "Hello, Hello?" People see cable lines and phone lines as two different things.

Armstrong's dream of transforming AT&T into a futuristic communications supermarket offering TV, local and long-distance telephone, and Internet services turned into a nightmare. As he admitted in the *Wall Street Journal*, "The numbers are against you."

The result was a lot of debt and not a lot of business. It also resulted in the breakup of the company into four parts: wireless, broadband, business, and consumer (line extension strikes again). If it couldn't work as one entity, will it work as four entities? That is a $90 billion question, currently what AT&T is worth. But we don't doubt that C. Michael Armstrong will give it his all because it's what *Business Week* describes as "Armstrong's last stand."

 **Reality is critical in a competitive world.**

When AT&T was forced out of its monopoly into the competitive world, management did not have a sense of reality. Their business had changed from one where strategy was based on "What do we want to do?" to one where they should have asked, "What can we do?"

Conquering the computer industry was a sure example of what they wanted to do. Becoming an any-distance supplier of voice, data, and video was another example. Both ignored the reality of what their competitors would let them do. Both ignored the power of specialists in the marketplace. They are competing with companies that concentrate on specific activities or products. The market perceives these companies as experts and as having more knowledge and expertise than they sometimes deserve.

Conversely, the market seldom perceives the generalist as having expertise in many fields of endeavor no matter how good he or she may be. To dramatize this point, the following illustrates what AT&T was up against:

- AT&T PCs versus IBM's PC, Compaq, and Apple.
- AT&T's minicomputers versus DEC and IBM minicomputers.
- AT&T's WorldNet versus AOL and Yahoo!
- AT&T's cable telephone versus the Baby Bells.

These powerful brands quickly ran over AT&T's entries. My advice to Ma Bell is to get real.

 Focus is critical in a competitive world.

Management demands substantial increases in annual sales and profits, even when companies are in markets that show no overall growth. Predictably, to meet these targets, companies offer more varieties and flavors. Or they branch out into other markets. Or they acquire other firms or products. Or they set up joint ventures.

Whether you call this expansion process "line extension," "diversification," or "synergy," it's the process itself—the urge to grow—that causes companies to become unfocused. While growth might be an admirable result of other initiatives, the pursuit of growth for its own sake is a serious strategic error.

Keeping a Focus

A successful company usually starts out highly focused on an individual product, service, or market. Over time, the company becomes unfocused and loses its sense of direction by offering too many products and services for too many markets at too many price levels. It doesn't know where it's going or why. Its mission statement loses its meaning.

At first, everything seems to be going well. The initial product or service turns out to be a big winner. The company has momentum and great expectations. The stock is taking off like a rocket.

But success creates something else: the opportunity to branch out in many directions. The halls are filled with anticipation and excitement. There's a sense of "We can do anything." Well, now that the marketplace has demonstrated that this is certainly not the case, let's go back and introduce the discipline of focus into AT&T.

First Focus Communications

AT&T is a communications company. They always have been; they always will be. Any movement away from this is doomed to failure. They learned this the hard way with ventures into computers (as did Xerox). Getting into wireless made sense because it was a communications business. Cable television is questionable—in its present one-way form, it is a television business, not a communications business. AT&T is trying to change that perception by introducing an "inside" communications word. They are changing from AT&T

Cable Services (television) to AT&T Broadband (what's that?). This might be a tough one to pull off.

Because of its many forms, "communications" is a broad concept. What's required here is yet a little more focus.

Second Focus Business

When AT&T lost its local consumer business to the Baby Bells, it was time to take stock on where they should focus their efforts now that their local business was gone. They still controlled a lot of long distance, still had an amazing national network, and still had satellites and fiber-optic cable and 40,000 networking professionals to make it all work. They had an enviable position in the business services market because these are all the things big companies need.

My advice would have been to protect their long-distance consumer business as best they could but to focus on their business customers as a long-term goal. This would have meant linking private data networks with the Internet while improving security capabilities. But most of all, it would preclude any expensive efforts to get back into the local, consumer business. Forget it, that business is gone and difficult to get back. The Baby Bells will do everything they can to hang on to it.

The AT&T strategy should not be everything for everybody. The strategy should focus on becoming *the leader in global business communications*.

An Interesting Analogy

IBM was faced with a similar problem. Its mainframe business was taking a hit as downsizing increased among their big enterprise customers. But rather than break apart, Lou Gerstner decided to find a way to take advantage of IBM's size and technological depth. He started to talk about "integrated computing" as IBM's unique strength. After all, what company could put all the pieces together other than IBM? Reason: Only IBM, the one-time hardware king, made most of the pieces. All its main competitors were only good at certain things.

The result is that, today, IBM's hottest product isn't a product, it's their services division that is leaving rivals in the dust. IBM's Global Services Division is proving to be the company's savior. While sales for the rest of Big Blue are barely increasing, the services division is averaging more than 10 percent sales growth annually.

This raises an interesting question. Could AT&T become a major player in integrated communications? Their big business customers sure could use some help in putting together the complex global communications networks that digital technology is making possible. It's just a thought, but it could be a big business. After all, who could better put all the pieces together?

 ## Differentiation is critical in a competitive world.

AT&T isn't alone in trying to serve the world of business communications. There's WorldCom, for example, trying very hard to take AT&T's business. Quest is a long-distance upstart. And many other specialists are doing one thing or another. The burning question that AT&T needs to answer is, Why should a customer do business with AT&T instead of its competitors? That question has never been effectively answered.

Interestingly, I had a crack at answering this question some years ago. What prompted my visit to AT&T was a series of major service disruptions in the early 1990s. AT&T received a lot of negative press and was concerned about the company's reputation. The first thing was to ask to see their research on the problem. They had both tracking and perceptual studies. Their tracking studies showed some dips but no residual damage to their business or reputation. But a look at their attribute research, saw a serious problem vis-à-vis their major competitors, MCI and Sprint.

Not Enough Difference

At the time, AT&T had over a 60 percent market share in long distance, but their "overall quality" score, while high, was not as high as their market share would indicate. They had a 10 percent lead over their competitors. That's not a big difference.

The numbers really narrowed when I looked at the "worth what you paid for" scores. For all practical purposes, Sprint actually tied AT&T. That was pretty good for a company with only a 9 percent market share.

And on the attribute of "call quality," once again Sprint was neck and neck with only a single point difference. I suspected that this was a result of their fiber-optic technology pitch.

AT&T did a little better on "customer assistance" with the others hanging in there about 10 points behind.

Sprint actually passed AT&T on "Billing Quality" with a 5-point advantage. MCI once again brought up the rear.

AT&T's competitors might not be getting the business, but they were getting the perceptions.

The Key Attribute

When you looked at the all important attribute of "reliability," one could see that Sprint was very close to AT&T with only a 3-point differential. Even MCI's score wasn't that far off the lead. And these competitors had only a fraction of expertise, facilities, and experience of good old Ma Bell.

In looking at all these numbers, it was hard to miss the observation that AT&T had allowed its competition to get very close to them in perceptions. This is why things had become so price driven. The market was tending to view the category more and more as a commodity. This was not good news for AT&T.

One could ask why Sprint, in particular, has made so much progress in creating a favorable perception. A look at their advertising pointed to the answer. Sprint had a focus in their "Fiber Optics" program. People were obviously impressed with their technological approach, which is why they were so close to AT&T in perceptions. AT&T was taking their technological lead for granted.

But why the market share success of MCI? Well, MCI also had a focus. From day one, they made "Low Price" their positioning idea. And if the market doesn't see a lot of differences, this is a good strategy. At the time, their low-price move "Friends and Family" only extended this strategy in an interesting way.

What Is AT&T's Difference?

During this period, AT&T spent a lot of money talking about being "the right choice." But the perception numbers pointed to the logical conclusion that this idea wasn't working. AT&T was much more vulnerable to the price moves of the competition than it should have been and the technological strength of the company wasn't being communicated effectively. People didn't see the differences between AT&T and the likes of MCI and Sprint.

I felt that they should move on to answer more succinctly just why they were the "right choice." What made them different?

The answer to the question should have been reliability. That was the leader's most important attribute, especially with the technological superiority that AT&T possessed.

That led to the next issue: how to convince their customers that AT&T was more reliable. In looking for answers, I asked about the main problems they encountered with their highly vaunted network that had millions of miles of fiber-optic cable. One engineer answered quickly, "That's easy, a backhoe." They went on to explain that with so much buried cable, someone digging could inadvertently cut a line. And with the volume going through that cable, a big hunk of, say, Atlanta, would lose its service.

I asked, "What happens then?"

An Amazing Piece of Technology

With that, they demonstrated on their famous network videowall exactly what happens when a break occurs. Instantly, a program called "Fastar" automatically re-routes all calls around the break. In a matter of minutes (now it's seconds), every call is on its way to its destination. And here's the stunning statistic. That system, with the extra cable lines, took 5 years and cost about $13 billion to install. In essence, they had a "self-restoring network" that no one knew anything about. (Let's see MCI and Sprint match that.) It was about as dramatic a demonstration of AT&T's reliability that you could ever cook up.

But to the folks at AT&T, it was just another feature of the AT&T network. It was no big deal. This was a big mistake. I recommended that they make this a big deal by making it inherent in the network itself. In other words, drop the name Fastar (it sounded like a racehorse) and begin to talk at great length about *AT&T's Self-Restoring Network*. And, more importantly, launch a massive PR and advertising program about this unique and expensive piece of engineering aimed at making the network the most reliable in the world.

They would be telling a story that has never been told effectively. By so doing, they would take AT&T beyond being the "right choice" to being "the reliable choice." It would begin to separate them from their lesser and cheaper competitors, especially in the minds of their all-important business customers with critical phone and data traffic that they can't afford to have interrupted. In addition, all the new technology being introduced only tended to cause more confusion among business customers. Who better to trust to help them with it than the most reliable one?

It Never Happened

Despite these efforts, I could never move the powers-that-be to focus on their unique and untold reliability story. Their self-restoring network is still a well-kept secret. As often happens in huge corporations, there were too many people and organizations with their own agendas. And these recommendations challenged a number of them by encouraging them to change their plans.

Eventually, new management arrived and billions were spent on becoming everything for everybody via voice, data ad video. Big, unattainable ideas replaced simple, attainable ideas.

CHAPTER 6

Levi Strauss

Ignoring Competition Is Bad for Your Business

In 1853, Levi Strauss opened a dry goods store in San Francisco. His customers were mostly gold rush miners. After a local prospector told him that the miners were having a hard time finding pants that could last through a hard day's work, Strauss made a pair of pants out of canvas. These rugged pants were an instant hit. Eventually Strauss replaced the canvas with denim, colored them blue, and reinforced them with copper rivets.

In 1873, Strauss produced the first pair of Levi's Patent Riveted 501 waist-high overalls (501 was a lot number). These pants quickly became the standard attire of lumberjacks, cowboys, railroad workers, oil drillers, and farmers. By the 1950s, it was the standard attire of American youth (James Dean wore them). In the 1960s, the company introduced women's clothing and expanded overseas.

Levi's First Mistake

In 1971, the corporation was taken public and now they had Wall Street or the "How do you plan to grow?" demons on their back. They decided to become more than just a jeans company. They became an apparel company and quickly fell into the everything-for-everybody trap as they bought Perry Ellis, Oxford Suits, and Koret, a maker of women's clothing.

While their nonjeans business turned out to be a big mistake, luckily the jeans business continued to grow. At its peak, in 1981, 502 million pairs of jeans were sold in the U.S. market alone. Obviously, a lot more than just cowboys and kids were wearing them.

Concerned about its business and the family tradition, the Haas family, who were the descendants of Levi Strauss, began to take a more active role in managing the company, went private, and sold off all their nonjeans business. Wall Street was off their back, and they were again focusing on the pants business. To emphasize this, they introduced the very successful Dockers line in 1987. But as the 1990s approached, blue jeans, for generations the uniform of rebels and conformists alike, started to fade from the fashion forefront. U.S. sales dropped from that lofty 502 million pants to 387 million in 1989. Big trouble was on the horizon.

The Rise of Competition

As jeans hit their stride as a fashion mainstay, a lot of new competitors also hit the stores. The VF Corporation had three brands—Lee, Wrangler, and Rustler. Store brands were launched by JCPenney, Sears, and the Gap. There were also the designer jeans of Calvin Klein and Tommy Hilfiger. And a youth-oriented brand from Italy called Diesel entered the scene in Europe. By the time the dust settled, consumers were looking at names like Junco, Mudd, Arizona, Fubu, Badge, Union Bar, Canyon River Blues,

Bongo, Faded Glory, and others that even Levi executives may not have been aware of.

Suddenly, Levi's was up to its red tag logo in competitors. This put enormous pressure on distribution as shelf space became more difficult to protect. While their Dockers brand continued its strong showing, Levi's started to make big mistakes in the jeans business. And, making mistakes in a competitive world can be costly.

In 1990, Levi's had 48.2 percent of the jeans category. Lee and Wrangler had 22.1 percent, "Other" had 26.5 percent, and "Private Label" had 3.2 percent. In 1998, Levi's share was down to 25.0 percent, Lee and Wrangler had 31.9 percent, Other had 22.7 percent and Private Label had climbed to 20.5 percent of the business. The world had turned upside down for the people who invented jeans. Their leadership had evaporated as did a lot of their sales. That's trouble with a capital "T."

What went wrong? A lot of things helped their competitors gain enormous ground. It is a rare example of a company that took its leadership for granted. It is also a rare example of living in your own world.

 **Not establishing your leadership helps your competition.**

Early on, when Levi's was in a strong leadership position, they should have clearly planted their flag at the top of the mountain. Leadership is the most powerful way to differentiate a brand because it's the most direct way to establish the brand's credentials. And credentials are the collateral you put up to guarantee the performance of that brand. Americans love underdogs, but they bet on the winners.

When you're on top, you have to make sure the marketplace knows it. Too many companies take their leadership for granted (Levi's for one) and never exploit it. All this does is keep the door open for competition. If you get a chance, slam the door in your competitors' faces.

The Cola Strategy

In one way, the inventor of jeans should have emulated those folks in Atlanta who invented the cola.

Some years ago, when Pepsi really began to raise its head and its share, Coke unfurled one of the most powerful expressions of leadership ever seen in the business. They created the ultimate put-down with three words: *The real thing*. What that did was establish leadership while questioning their competitor's legitimacy. Who wants to drink a fake cola? Or just a me-too?

Psychologically, people always want the original, the first, and the inventor. We tend to give that person or product more than they might deserve because, deep down, we suspect (rightly or wrongly) that they know more and are all the better for it.

What Levi's should have done was to end every commercial with a powerful statement of fact that would have made all their competitors second-class citizens:

Original Levi's.
Everything else is a copy.

That would have forced their customers to ask themselves a tough question as they stood in front of those racks of look-alike jeans: "Do I want the real thing or an imitation thing?" If the price wasn't too far out of line, most would probably go for the real thing. (Ironically, the European business of Levi's was wildly successful by positioning the jeans as "original.")

Of course, it wouldn't have hurt if they had continued to explain why a pair of Levi's was better than those "copies" out there—construction, fabric, rivets, something. Because of their leadership, people would have tended to believe whatever they said about why they were better.

Inside Levi's, people thought that the name alone was enough. But, the name alone is never enough. Sure, Hertz could just use their name. Hey, they invented the rent-a-car business years and years ago. But they constantly remind their customers about who is the leader and the also-rents:

Hertz.
There's Hertz and not exactly.

That's how you stay on top of that mountain. But other missteps were in play for Levi's.

 **Not keeping your costs in line helps your competitors.**

When Robert Haas led the LBO of Levi Strauss in 1996, he placed one of the world's most successful brands in the hands of four people: himself, an uncle, and two cousins. A Harvard MBA who had worked for the Peace Corps and McKinsey before joining Levi Strauss, he had been lionized in the business press for applying his enlightened management practices to an old-line clothing manufacturer. He was intent on showing that a company driven by social values can outperform a company that is hostage to profits alone. To him, a company had to have a purpose beyond making money. That's a nice idea, but in our world of killer competition, it's not realistic. Here's what happened.

- *"Made in the U.S."* The Haas family didn't want to close plants even though their costs were 25 percent above their competitors' costs (because of offshore manufacturing). They figured that "Made in the U.S." was a big deal. They didn't notice that their competitors were having no trouble selling jeans that were not made in the United States. As a result, Levi's prices got too high and too close to the designer crowd. This led retailers to give more space to Calvin, Tommy, and others where they could make more money. And their lesser me-too competitors were able to exploit the big difference in price. People will pay a little more for perceived value just as long as you're in the ballpark. They have to feel that they are getting their money's worth. While Levi's prices started to bump up toward the designer level, they didn't offer the prestige that Calvin and others offered. Levi's got squeezed between the fancy guys and the cheap guys.

- *"Serve our customers better."* Bob Haas figured reengineering was the ticket to getting around the pricing problem. Levi's asked hundreds of insiders to redesign the company, and 100 Andersen consultants came in to help design a Customer Service Supply Chain. Six hundred job descriptions were rewritten. Endless meetings were held and confusion set in.

By the time the board of directors stepped in to put an end to the nonsense, the company had spent a stunning $850 million. And nothing was improved. For example, a few hundred million of this sum was spent for five large new distribution centers in the United States and Europe. These high-tech centers were so poorly designed that they actually increased Levi's distribution expenses and made the company less competitive. In addition, they were located and designed to receive goods from the U.S. Levi's plants. This made it more difficult to close these high-cost plants without creating chaos. The company is still feeling the effect of this mistake.

The retailers, the people actually meant to benefit from all this, shook their heads in disbelief. In an April 12, 1999 *Fortune* article on Levi's troubles, a buyer at one of Levi's major accounts was reported to say, "The re-engineering changes had us confused as hell. One minute there was no customer service, the next minute they'd overdo it." The same article pointed out that as far as restocking basic product, JCPenney's standard was 20 days; Levi's average in 1998 was 27 days.

So much for all those consultants (more on these folks in Chapter 13).

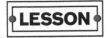 Inside thinking is good for competition.

Haas's efforts at a utopian management experiment created an inward-looking company. He envisioned Levi Strauss as a company where a factory worker's voice was as likely to be heard as the CEO's. All too many people, however, were quick to register their personal agendas. By trying to involve everybody in the decision-making process, no decisions were made in a timely way. It took too much time to react to marketplace change.

Bob Haas actually drew an organizational chart for use in employee presentations that turned the familiar pyramid upside down to illustrate how the people "closest" to the business would be making the decisions and management would be there to coach and assist them. This concept of empowerment was so confusing to people that it paralyzed decision making.

To make the situation worse, many initiatives forced the company to spend a great amount of time staring at its navel instead of its competition. Compensation plans were changed so that one-third of executives' bonuses reflected their ability to manage "aspirationally." Haas assigned 80 task forces to make the company more "aspirational." One of these sent a 25-page questionnaire to 17,000 employees. A diversity focus group organized off-site sessions to discuss racial and gender stereotypes. Other groups discussed their vulnerabilities, shared their deepest fears, and even composed their obituaries. It was new-age thinking run amok.

It was no wonder that all this led to some big trouble.

Losing Touch

As the denim market changed, Levi's people were too busy going to meetings. Kids started telling retailers that the legs were too narrow. Big retailers created their own jeans with legs as wide as 23 inches. JCPenney, Sears, Tommy Hilfiger, and others got into the act. Some got as wide as 40 inches. Through it all, Levi Strauss kept on pushing 16-inch-wide legs. Levi's jeans were rapidly becoming uncool.

Even the highly successful Dockers line was affected. While everyone was off in some meeting or other, they missed one of the biggest trends in the khaki market: wrinkle-resistant pants. Dockers stayed put. Sales collapsed.

As specialty stores gained popularity with the youth, Levi's continued to sell almost exclusively to out-of-favor department stores. Discounters became big players but Levi's didn't have a low-cost brand with which to play (VF, the big competitor, did).

When a company spends a large proportion of its time on inside-out thinking, only bad things happen. A good marketer thinks outside in.

Bob Haas tried very hard to do the right thing. Yet all the benefits of his programs ended up helping Levi's competitors more than they helped Levi's. It was greatly disappointing to many senior managers that after a track record from 1985 to 1996 within the top 1 percent of the American business (almost 50 percent compound growth in profits and a nearly 50 times increase in the stock value) the emphasis on creating a successful business first and doing "good" second would be totally reversed with disastrous results.

Levi's Future

All the mistakes I've just outlined are not news to Levi Strauss. They have all been duly registered and the company is taking steps to redefine its mission from being a responsible commercial success to becoming the "casual apparel authority."

Once again, organizational changes are sweeping through the company. They realize that kids don't wear the same jeans as their parents. And they see that the marketplace has segmented calling for a "multibrand" strategy. My question is, have these realizations come too late? After all, Levi's multibrand strategy is something its big competitor, VF, has done for years. And is it really multibrand?

At present, they are using tags of different colors to differentiate the levels of Levi's: silver (best), red (the original 501), orange (not so good). But a tag does not a brand make. The brand is still Levi's. And if Levi's is the "original" jeans that Ralph Lauren wore when he was a kid, how can you change them very much? When Coke changed its original formula and came out with a new, sweeter cola for the kids, it was a disaster. If they weren't the original, they were nothing. Luckily, it didn't take but a few months for Coca-Cola to become "classic" again with the original formula. Let the kids buy wide-legged jeans. When they grow up, chances are they will come back to the "original" if Levi's has patience and keeps reminding them they are wearing silly-shaped copies.

But it looks as if Levi's doesn't have much patience. They have launched Red Line jeans for the kids. But to maintain their coolness, they go out of their way to hide the Levi's identity. They even have their headquarters in a different place. Then why do it? If you keep it as a separate brand, it just becomes one of a pack of many kids' brands. They admit they won't make much money on this effort but hope the jeans will have a "halo effect" that will seep into Levi's other lines. (How does that happen?)

The multibrand strategy they should pursue is that of Levi's (the original jeans), Dockers (no. 1 in khakis), and Slates (when it's time to dress up). If they can keep those brands healthy, strong, and well positioned, the free ride their competitors have had for many years will be over.

CHAPTER 7

Crest Toothpaste

Look, Ma, No Leadership

In *Television's Classic Commercials: The Golden Years, 1948–1958* (New York: Hastings House, 1971), Lincoln Diamant offered this summary of a well-known spot for Procter & Gamble's Crest brand: "The car door flies open, a six-year-old girl in pigtails dances across the suburban lawn clutching her dental 'report card'—and suddenly, with the immortal 'Look, Ma! No cavities!' the fluoride toothpaste era was born."

Actually, the truly pivotal event happened in 1955, when Crest debuted as the first toothpaste brand containing fluoride, a substance found to prevent tooth decay. Stannous fluoride, which Crest used in a patented mixture it called "Fluoristan," promised to literally alter the appearance of the human race. Up to that time, loss of teeth—which tended to speed the process of aging, both physically and psychologically—had been a fact of life for people of a certain age.

Now Crest promised to change that fact.

The Battle over Leadership

When Crest arrived on the scene, Colgate-Palmolive's Colgate brand dominated the market, followed by Pepsodent and Ipana. The latter two brands would all but disappear, and the true battle would be between Crest and Colgate.

The rivalry bore similarities to that between Ford and General Motors (GM) in the car business and R.J. Reynolds and Philip Morris in the cigarette industry. In each case, one company came to dominate the market in the early part of the century—Ford, Reynolds, and Colgate—and each was surrounded by a variety of lesser lights. In the case of Philip Morris and Crest, at least, the greater challenge came from a dark horse, a brand that rapidly shot from the bottom of the market to the top. Each of the three challengers—GM, Philip Morris, and Crest—would ultimately unseat the market leader, and in future decades, each of the three industries would be a battleground on which the two leading companies fought for preeminence. In *The 22 Immutable Laws of Marketing* (HarperCollins, 1993), it's called the law of duality.

The Fluoride Edge

What gave Crest the edge over Colgate was fluoride, along with Procter & Gamble's ability to promote it. For years, studies had shown that residents of communities where sodium fluoride appeared naturally in the drinking water had far fewer cavities and other dental problems than people whose water supply lacked the chemical. P&G scientists went to work on a formula to incorporate it in a toothpaste, but this was not as simple as one might think because other ingredients in the paste reacted with sodium fluoride.

The work took place at Indiana University, where three chemists—Joseph Muhler, Harry Day, and William Nebergall—tested some 500 compounds over the course of nine years. Muhler, a graduate student in one of Day's classes, took the lead. In 1997,

Day, the only one of the three still alive, told Vince Staten of the *Louisville Courier-Journal*, "Muhler sat on the front row. Most of the students didn't give a hoot (about chemistry). They just wanted to fill teeth. But he got interested. I had told him when he wanted a project to work on, he could compare different fluorides, but I'd be surprised if there was any difference."

Ultimately, Muhler discovered stannous fluoride, which worked where sodium fluoride had failed. Crest was born. The cavity-fighting qualities of the ingredient figured heavily in Crest advertising, including the "Look, Ma!" commercial. After the little girl told her mother that she had "no cavities," the mother said, "Golly, what a difference that Crest toothpaste has made," and the voice-over announced, "Yes, Crest is the toothpaste that works, because Crest is the toothpaste with Fluoristan, a special fluoride formula. Fluoride, you know, is the decay fighter dentists use."

The Fluoride Victory

Despite these impressive claims, however—which, unlike similar claims surrounding alleged miracle ingredients in other brands, could be backed up by evidence—Crest remained at a 10 percent market share. This wasn't bad for a brand that had appeared only a few years earlier, but P&G executives knew that they had a technological breakthrough on their hands. They also knew that Colgate, which soon introduced its own stannous fluoride brand, Cue, stood a good chance of eliminating the small market share Crest had managed to eke out. Meanwhile, a P&G executive—destined to become president of the company—was working quietly behind the scenes, engineering a coup that would affect the future of Crest far more than any advertising could.

John Smale, then associate advertising manager, petitioned the ADA to officially recognize the decay-fighting properties of Crest and its stannous fluoride. Smale believed that such recognition would tip the scale of public opinion in Crest's favor. The problem was that the ADA had never endorsed a toothpaste brand, and it wasn't inclined to do so. Only after years of petitioning, along with the presentation of mounting evidence, did the ADA finally issue its statement of approval. This statement would become a staple of Crest advertising thenceforth. Thus Diamant observed that the ADA "came to the creative man's rescue, with the immortal line: 'Crest has been shown to be an effective decay-preventing dentifrice that can be of significant value when used in a conscientiously applied program of oral hygiene and regular professional care.'"

Thanks to this endorsement, Crest soon controlled fully a third of the toothpaste market, and it embarked on more than 35 years of dominance.

The Fluoride Problem

But nothing stays the same in war or marketing.

Local communities starting putting fluoride in their drinking water and children's cavities began to disappear. In 1960, the average mouth had 15 cavities. By 1987, there were only 3 cavities to fill. The cavity prevention concept was losing its power. This posed a problem for Crest because as cavities disappeared, niche brands started to become more successful and Crest's market share began to decline. You had the "nostalgic" niche of baking soda toothpaste. You had the "natural" niche of Tom's of Maine toothpaste. You had the "tobacco stain" niche of Topol. You had the "sensitive teeth" niche of Sensodyne. In addition, you had the rise of cosmetic toothpastes such as Ultra Brite, Close-Up, and Aquafresh. They whitened your teeth or freshened your breath while you were brushing. You looked good and your breath smelled better.

Crest at the Crossroads

All this activity created a dilemma for Crest. Should they try to become everything for everybody? Should they launch a mouthwash

Crest? Or a whitening Crest? Or a baking soda Crest? Or a sensitive teeth Crest? Changes like these would weaken their strong therapeutic position of protecting teeth and also could open the door for their therapeutic twin, Colgate.

The other problem they faced was the "Use it or lose it" dilemma. Aim once had a 10 percent share of the toothpaste market by positioning themselves as the "good tasting toothpaste." Their theme was simple: "Hey, mom, kids will brush longer because they love the taste." But Aim fell into the everything-for-everybody trap with an antitartar version and a mint-gel version. Today they have a 0.8 share. If Procter & Gamble wanted to play in the cosmetic game, they needed to pursue the Honda/Acura strategy of launching different brands into different segments. When you try to become everything for everybody, you often become nothing. What's a Chevrolet? It's a large, small, cheap, expensive, car, truck, sports car. It's nothing.

How about Stages?

A suggestion once floated around P&G about launching a Crest for different stages of life. It is the Pampers strategy: newborn, infant, crawler, and walker. But what this ignored was that Pampers stages cover about 3 years in a child's life. Crest would have to cover 70 years: kids (taste), young adults (mouthwash), seniors (sensitive teeth formula). And the stages were already taken: kids (Aim), young adults (Aquafresh), grown-ups (Crest), seniors (Sensodyne). This obviously wouldn't have worked.

So, what should Crest have done? Here's where they learned some painful lessons because they didn't do what they should have done.

 Sometimes you've got to evolve your position.

First and foremost, Crest should always be on the serious, therapeutic side of the toothpaste market. That's where they are in the mind of their prospects. No mouthwash, no whitening, only serious tooth care technology. The natural evolution of Crest would be to move from "cavity prevention" to becoming the "pioneer in tooth care." Unfortunately, they never quite saw this as a way to go. They continued to tinker with different forms of Crest.

Just studying tooth trends would have told them how to evolve:

- Cavities are declining.
- People are living longer and keeping their teeth longer.
- Tartar control and gum disease are becoming more important.

So let's take a look at tartar control, which turned out to be another painful lesson learned the hard way.

   Never lose your corporate memory.

P&G, to their credit, launched tartar control toothpaste in 1985. But they never got the competitive bounce they received with their fluoride launch. One reason is they appeared to have forgotten what they did so successfully in 1955. There was no drama such as "Triumph over Tartar" in their advertising. They simply talked about how less plaque would mean easier teeth cleaning at the dentist. This is a trivial matter to most people.

The story that should have been told is:

- Cavities, thanks in part to Crest, are less of a problem today.
- What is a big problem today is petrified plaque or tartar.
- Tartar can lead to gum problems and loss of teeth.

They also forgot to put a magic ingredient into the story. With the fluoride story, they had "Fluoristan." With the tartar story, they should have introduced "Tartastan." There was no such introduction.

One reason this may have happened was that the team in charge wasn't around more than 30 years ago when Crest was launched. There was no corporate memory of their formula for success.

In addition, Crest never put the same kind of focus on this story. This was just one of the many different versions they were advertising. There was only one kind of Crest in 1955.

Finally, Colgate had learned its lesson from what they probably described internally as the "fluoride fiasco." They quickly responded to the Crest introduction with advertising that pointed to greater tartar reduction with their tartar control product. They gave Crest no running room.

That was unfortunate. But what happened next was real trouble.

 **Never give a strong competitor an edge.**

Tooth trends indicated the natural progression in the tooth-care category: cavity prevention, tartar control, and gingivitis protection. Crest was there for the first two but the real battle was going to be over gingivitis. The first one to nail all three tooth care benefits had a shot at becoming the winner. Crest knew this as did Colgate. But someone, somewhere in P&G, was willing to take the risk of letting Colgate grab the gingivitis edge. They gave Colgate this edge by not being first and by not quickly blocking Colgate's efforts with a product of their own. Someone on the case once told me that it was a R&D problem. My advice would have been to quickly find better R&D people.

The result was that the first into the market with all three attributes (cavity prevention, tartar control, gingivitis protection) was Colgate's Total. The success of this product enabled Colgate to climb back into the lead after spending three decades in second place. Not only does it speak to their perseverance, but it's the kind of turnaround that rarely occurs in this competitive world.

Somewhere at Colgate, a smiling product manager ran into an office clutching some market share numbers and proudly announced, "Look, boss, we're the leader."

CHAPTER 8

Burger King

Always under New Management

In an article entitled, "A Tarnished Crown," *Newsweek* (November 13, 2000) summed up a lot of trouble at America's also-ran burger chain:

> The perennial No. 2 in the burger wars is struggling with a menu of problems, from sluggish sales to ineffective ads to a boycott led by media-savvy Al Sharpton . . . Now Burger King is searching for its seventh CEO in eleven years. It is also likely to replace its advertising agency. Sales at established U.S. stores have been down thanks in part to a limp ad campaign featuring the less than memorable slogan "Got the urge?"

Needless to say, there's trouble in Burger King Town.

The Early Years

Burger King and the famous Whopper were born in the late 1950s. Their timing couldn't have been better. The 1960s marked the early years of the fast-food industry, including restaurant chains and franchises. The pace of the American lifestyle quickened with the development of suburbia, automobiles, and television, and the climate was ripe for convenient, affordable food-service establishments. The fast-food market grew explosively during the late 1960s and early 1970s, and competition was fierce as restaurants fought for market share and supremacy.

The Battle for Leadership

Burger King was one of the largest restaurant chains in the United States, and the company was well on its way to becoming a fast-food leader. The company understood the importance of advertising, and by the late 1960s, it was large enough to afford slots on network television. Much of Burger King's advertising efforts through the 1960s revolved around the Whopper, the chain's most popular item. One Whopper campaign used the jingle, "The bigger the burger, the better the burger." Another early marketing endeavor used the slogan, "It takes two hands" (to handle a Whopper).

Successful advertising slogans were not enough to help Burger King with its biggest concern. Though Burger King restaurants opened at an ambitious rate, the company could not afford to continue at a similar pace without additional capital. Attempts to take the company public failed, so when Pillsbury Company approached Burger King with a proposition to merge, Burger King accepted, believing that Pillsbury could provide the solution to its financial problems.

McDonald's Breaks Away

Following the merger, however, Pillsbury cut back expansion plans, much to Burger King's dismay. Competition, specifically McDonald's, surged past, and Burger King could do little but watch.

In 1970, Burger King opened 167 new stores. But McDonald's opened 294 stores and launched the "You Deserve a Break Today" campaign. The next year, Burger King dropped to 107 new openings while McDonald's added a stunning 384 stores.

The game was over. McDonald's had become the market leader by leaps and bounds. Burger King was forced to settle for second place.

"Have It Your Way"

The leadership issue settled, Burger King began to act like a good number two: They attacked the leader. In 1973, they launched a successful marketing campaign that pinpointed McDonald's weakness of being a highly automated and inflexible hamburger machine. The new campaign focused on the changing tastes of individual customers. Here was their promise to the customer:

> Hold the pickles, hold the lettuce. Special orders won't upset us.
> All we ask is that you let us serve it your way.

The "Have It Your Way" campaign was a rousing success, and the slogan persisted for decades.

But this was just warming up. As the 1980s rolled around, things really got competitive.

Comparative Advertising

In 1982, Jeff Campbell, who was executive vice president of marketing, brilliantly raised the ante with some very competitive programs. There was "Broiling Not Frying" and the "Battle of the Burgers." For the first time in the restaurant category, advertising was used to make four points of comparison: (1) The Burger King Whopper sandwich beat McDonald's Big Mac and Wendy's Single in blind taste tests, (2) flame-broiling was preferred over frying, (3) "Have it your way" was preferred to accepting it their way, and (4) the regular size burgers at Burger King were bigger than those at McDonald's.

One of the initial ads, known internally as the "Lea Thompson" spot, opened with a close-up of a Whopper and the voice-over saying, "An important message from Burger King." Thompson then was seen sitting in a leather chair in front of a fire. She states,

> For a long time there was McDonald's, Burger King and Wendy's. Some things change, some don't. But the Whopper beat the Big Mac in a consumer test of both burgers. As a result, there will still be McDonald's, Burger King and Wendy's . . . but not necessarily in that order.

The campaign continued throughout 1983, first focusing for a few weeks on "Broiling Beat Frying" and then inaugurating a four-month campaign based on the phrase "Millions Switched." This touted that millions actually had switched restaurants. The claim was supported by data from restaurant industry consults at CREST, a research firm in Rosemont, Illinois. This aggressive advertising included a spot featuring a former McDonald's family disguised in Groucho Marx glasses and mustaches because they had switched and could no longer show their faces.

Successive advertising again emphasized the advantages of flame-broiled burgers over fried ones from McDonald's and Wendy's. The campaign used on-camera talent that included a family of cavemen, a toddler, and the 1980s' TV star Emanuel Lewis. Dempsey stated, "In one of our new spots, we say that since people from early caveman to modern families have demonstrated a preference for flame-broiled meat, why should they ever settle for second best with fried burgers?"

One commercial featured girls at a slumber party discussing the advantages of Burger King's flame-broiled Double Burgers over McDonald's fried Quarter Pounders, and another one depicted a 1940s-style detective who recognized that the flame-broiled Double Burgers at Burger King spelled "double trouble" for fried burgers.

Hot Results

The results of the "Battle of the Burgers" campaign exceeded all expectations. Market share increased dramatically, and restaurant sales moved from $750,000 to more than $1 million in the following three years. Consumer ratings of Burger King improved sharply, while McDonald's and Wendy's showed declines. CREST found that, compared with the year before the campaign began, slightly more than 2 million consumers had switched to Burger King.

The real break for the "Battle of the Burgers" campaign came when both McDonald's and Wendy's brought legal action to have the ads taken off the air. Their actions provided publicity that gave the campaign an extra push toward success. The matter was later settled in a sealed agreement, but by then the campaign had run for three months, and it continued to run thereafter. The legal battle created extra awareness for Burger King customers as the dispute spilled over onto network news programs.

The Problems Begin

While all the lawsuits and animosity were good for business, they were bad for internal politics. Pillsbury was a conservative mid-Western company that expressed its concerns to their unruly subsidiary in Miami. It didn't take too much persuading. Suddenly

Burger King stopped being a good number two. They ceased attacking the leader. Instead, they started to look for what is called an "umbrella program" that would cover burgers, breakfast, and chicken. They figured that these kinds of programs worked for McDonald's ("You Deserve a Break Today" and "It's a Good Time for the Great Taste of McDonald's") so "why couldn't they work for us?"

So they launched "The Search for Herb," an embarrassing program that portrayed a nerd who was the only one never to have tasted a Whopper (this was a bomb).

Next up was "This is Burger King Town," although this made no sense because McDonald's had so many more outlets. Most places in the United States were "McDonald's Towns" (another bomb).

Then came "The Best Food for Fast Times." This also didn't ring true as highly automated McDonald's was perceived as being faster (yet another bomb).

All this raises an important lesson that number twos should never forget.

 **Number two has to stay on the attack.**

What Burger King learned the hard way was that umbrella programs only work for the leader. The only programs that work for nonleaders are attacking programs. Their own successful experience with "Have It Your Way," "The Battle of the Burgers," and "Broiling Not Frying" proved this point. They had McDonald's backpedaling and on the defensive. Once they took off the pressure, they allowed the leader to return to offense and set the agenda.

Even a look at Wendy's proved this thesis. They had great success with "Where's the Beef?" and "Hot 'n Juicy." And even though Dave Thomas is a wonderful spokesperson, none of their current work matches their early success of positioning Wendy's as having a better burger than those of McDonald's and Burger King.

Entering the Scene

In the late 1980s, Jeff Campbell asked myself and my former part-ner down to Miami to evaluate this umbrella versus attacking strat-egy issue and to come up with an answer to the "to attack or not to attack" dilemma.

Being the authors of *Marketing Warfare* (New York: McGraw-Hill, 1986), we voted on a resumption of their attacking strategy, but where and how to launch the attack was the question. So we took Campbell and his managers through the three basic principles of offensive warfare—the strategy that number two companies have to pursue.

Here, word for word, point for point, was what was presented to a small group of executives in a rather warm conference room in Miami. Basically it's an exercise in simple logic:

- What position are you in?

  Burger King is a strong No. 2 company and should practice the principles of offensive warfare.

  The leader, of course, is McDonald's who should play defense.

  Wendy's is a flanker and White Castle, among others, is a guerrilla.

  What are the principles of offensive warfare?

- Offensive principle No. 1:

  The main consideration is the strength of the leader's position.

  McDonald's is the leader.

- Where is McDonald's strong?

  "Speed of service" is where McDonald's is strong.

  Burger King should avoid attacking McDonald's strength.

- Offensive principle No. 2:

  Find a weakness in the leader's strength and attack at that point.

- What's the weakness in speed?

  At McDonald's, you have to take your burger their way, or be prepared to spend a lot of time in the penalty box.

  Over the years, you have exploited this weakness brilliantly with your "Have It Your Way" program.

  But times have changed.

- Speed of service has gotten more important relative to taste.

  One indication of that trend is the substantial increase in the percentage of drive-thru business.

  From 40 percent of the total in 1981 to 51 percent last year.

- It's time to look for another McDonald's strength to exploit.

  One obvious strength is kids, as symbolized by the Ronald McDonald character.

- What's the weakness in kids?

  The perception that McDonald's is a "kiddieland."

- In reality, most McDonald's restaurants have a strong kiddieland flavor as the entire front of many restaurants is a playground with swings and slides.

- Another indication of the strong relationship between kids and McDonald's is a new line of clothing being introduced by Sears and McDonald's.

  The name: McKids. (That was a bomb.)

- Offensive principle No. 3:

  Launch the attack on as narrow a front as possible.

- The obvious narrow front is burgers.

  Also, you should never overlook the fact that the sign on the restaurant says "Burger King."

  Even if you wanted to, you can't walk away from burgers.

- Where is Burger King strong?

  In a word, flame-broiling. This is an enormous strength that somehow needs to be coupled with the kiddieland weakness of McDonald's.

- This suggests an obvious two-part strategy:

  Part 1: Kiddieland. Rub their noses in the swings and slides at McDonald's.

  Part 2: Flame-broiling. When kids grow up, they prefer the flame-broiled taste of Burger King.

  This idea might seem obvious to you.

  But it's a fact of life that the easiest idea to overlook is the obvious one.

  Not only is the "grown up" idea obvious, but you've also used it before.

  But there are other ways to execute the "grow up" concept.

- Another possible execution is one we call "Rite of Passage" or situations like the first day at high school where younger kids are being instructed by older kids.

  This is a particularly powerful approach because it touches a basic human emotion: The moment of time when a kid is no longer a kid.

  It involves older kids pointing out to younger kids that McDonald's is for little kids who don't appreciate flame-broiled hamburgers.

- Would younger kids be offended by these commercials?

  We think not. No kid of any age, in our opinion, wants to be known as a kid. And grown-ups certainly don't want to hang out with little kids. (Unless the kids belong to them.) You might recognize this as the Pepsi-Cola strategy in reverse. Coke was the original and appealed to older folks. Pepsi sacrificed them to Coke and positioned themselves as the choice of the new generation. It was a big success.

All this was an attempt to get Jeff and his troops to understand a simple but fundamental lesson.

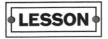 **Number two can't be what number one is.**

Not surprisingly, most number twos are convinced they have to emulate number one because it is bigger and more successful. The trick, however, is to be different, not the same. Our recommendation quickly raised another question: Does Burger King write off the kid market (a shocking idea for a family-oriented business)?

The answer to this question was a "no." Burger King had to draw a line between little kids and bigger kids. Once a kid graduates from swing sets and Ronald McDonald, they become Burger King kids or those who see themselves as more grown-up than those little guys going down the slides.

The point being made is that McDonald's owns the little kids and the chances of taking them away are slim at best. The basic principle is called sacrifice: You have to give up something to get something. To get the older kids, they had to give up the little kids. And yes, that meant removing all swing sets and little kids' promotions from the premises. (This also meant going to the franchisees and selling them this change.)

Nothing Changed but the Management

Change is hard to sell, especially when you have to sacrifice a piece of the market. These efforts were to no avail. Jeff Campbell ducked the decision by sending us to their advertising agency with the grow-up idea. Not surprisingly, they dumped all over it. Jeff decided not to fight, but to get promoted. Off he went to Pillsbury for a bigger job.

A parade of new managers and advertising agencies started to march through their Miami headquarters. As often is the case, each marched in with their own ideas on how to improve things. One bad ad campaign after another was launched. Here's a rundown of some ill-fated programs that were nothing but meaningless slogans:

"We Do It Like You'd Do It."
(People could hardly say this much less remember it.)

"Sometimes You've Gotta Break the Rules."
(Since when do hamburgers have rules?)

"Your Way. Right Way."
(Were they trying to sneak back to their 1973 idea?)

"Get Your Burger's Worth."
(If it's better, it shouldn't be cheaper.)

"Got the Urge?"
(Yes, to send out for a pizza.)

None of these attacked the leader's programs. So it can be accurately said that it has been almost 20 years since they ran their last strategically correct program ("Broiling Not Frying"). And on top of this they spent, or one could say wasted, a lot of promotional money trying to attract little kids with Kids Clubs and Walt Disney tie-ins. They continued to try to act as if they were number one, not number two. This is no way to succeed.

All this brings up another important lesson.

 **Changing management only confuses the troops.**

When you have had seven CEOs in 11 years and six advertising agencies in the past 20 years, it's no wonder that the natives are restless. All these people show up with their own agenda and new team members. They sweep around the company pointing out the problems of the previous regime and promising change for change's sake. But the troops have heard all this many times before. It's like an army with a succession of new generals, each with his own battle plan, all of which have failed.

So it's also no wonder that the company faces a revolt of franchisees, who are increasingly fed up with Burger King's owner, Diageo plc, the British conglomerate whose other brands include Guinness beer and Smirnoff vodka. And it's no wonder Burger

King now sells less food than it did five years ago, while its competitors are growing at five times the Burger King rate.

In that *Newsweek* article, Steven Lewis, the president of the National Franchisee Association that represents most of Burger King's 7,800 U.S. franchisees, did not have very nice things to say about the owner: "They're a distant, over controlling, overbearing parent that really has never taken the time to understand the business." Cutting loose from Diageo, Lewis insists, is "absolutely paramount for this brand to function and prosper."

Stand by, it looks like some more new management is in the wings.

Many years later Arby's, the roast beef sandwich chain, picked up the "grown-up" idea as they have been positioning themselves as the king of adult fast-food. Their current tagline: "Come to Arby's now that your tastes have grown up."

It just goes to show you that sooner or later, good ideas get discovered by someone.

CHAPTER

9

Firestone

Dead Brand Driving

When the Firestone flap erupted in 2000, there were 4,700 articles, press releases, and interviews about Ford Explorers rolling over, people dying or being injured, the dangers of tread separation, and many unanswered questions about what went wrong. Hundreds of millions of dollars in media space communicated one simple idea: Firestone made a lousy tire.

Can a brand overcome that kind of negative media? Can a media campaign, no matter how carefully crafted, counteract all that bad press?

Not likely.

Firestone was not even a strong brand when disaster struck. It was a second-tier brand behind Michelin, Goodyear, and Firestone's owner, Bridgestone. Strong brands have some goodwill in the bank and might have a fighting chance. Weak brands have little on which to draw. That's what makes Firestone's future so dicey. While their future is in doubt, they certainly have an impressive past.

The Early Years

It all started at the turn of the twentieth century when a 31-year-old investor and entrepreneur named Harvey S. Firestone seized on a new way of making carriage tires. He started with 12 employees in Akron, Ohio. Firestone, who was truly one of the pioneers in tire making, hung out with Thomas Edison and visited his botanical gardens. He was looking at, what else, rubber plants.

Firestone pioneered balloon, gum-dipped tires that were a breakthrough in car comfort and safety. They were a force in pioneering truck tires and at one time had half of the truck tonnage in the United States riding on Firestone tires. Firestone once ran a two-page advertisement in the *Saturday Evening Post* with the headline, "Ship by truck. The traffic motto of today and tomorrow." From what you see on today's highways, that was a wildly successful ad campaign.

During World War II, Firestone was a chief source of collapsible rubber rafts and floating bridges for American forces, as well as tires for trucks and jeeps.

The Racing Years

To put his tires to the ultimate test, Harvey Firestone entered and won the first Indianapolis 500. Over the years, this race at the fabled brickyard became a battle between Goodyear and Firestone. Every year, each would take turns proclaiming who won and the years that they won. And Firestone won a lot. Over the years, they collected 50 checkered flags and a lot of prestige, so much so that they went on to name a line of passenger car tires the "Firestone 500." They figured that the racing prestige would rub off. Unfortunately, the only thing that rubbed off was the tread of the tires.

The "500" Failures

Firestone's first experience with highly publicized tire failures happened in the mid- and late 1970s. The government forced a recall because of reports that 41 deaths and 65 injuries were caused by blowouts and other failures of the Firestone "500" tires.

In addition, they failed some of the government's safety tests. In all, about 14 million tires were recalled and Firestone's reputation was never the same. Goodyear became the dominant U.S. brand, and Firestone became a second-tier player. They had lost the most important race, the one for leadership.

But more than that, the financial repercussions of all those tire recalls led to Firestone's loss of independence and eventual purchase by a Japanese tire company with an amazingly similar name, Bridgestone. Thus in 1988, Harvey's name was moved into second place, as the company became Bridgestone/Firestone.

In the light of today's problems, it is ironic to note that Shojiro Ishibashi, the founder of Bridgestone, challenged his company to "Serve society with products of superior quality." And Harvey Firestone's mantra for his company was "Best today—still better tomorrow." One can only say that somewhere these two leaders are looking down on today's problems with a great deal of discomfort.

 **Two-name company names are not as good as one-name company names.**

When you merge two companies, it doesn't help matters if you become a two-brand name brand because both can suffer from the confused identity. Bridgestone is a big name in the Far East but a relative unknown in the U.S. tire market, even though they arrived in the United States in 1967.

Even their strong Japanese identity was clouded by their English-sounding name and their Italian-sounding tires (Potenza). Getting into the mind with one name is tough enough. Getting into the mind with two names is impossible. Will people ever say "PricewaterhouseCoopers?" It's not likely. They will just chop the Coopers off and continue to use the more powerful name in the merger, Pricewaterhouse.

Then there's the problem of having two brands in the name; if one of them gets into trouble, it will drag the other down with it. This is the current case of DaimlerChrysler. Chrysler is in trouble in Detroit, and their German associates feel the pain in Stuttgart. So it is with Bridgestone/Firestone. At long last, the Japanese part of the name is getting some awareness but it's of the negative kind.

Clearing Up the Confusion

Now might be the opportunity to deal with all the confusion by eliminating the "Firestone" name from the store signs and their corporate identity. Firestone is now a weak brand getting weaker. And it won't get any stronger as the lawsuits drag on and the negative publicity continues. Also, the original equipment manufacturer (OEM) business with U.S. carmakers such as Ford will certainly melt away as all the legal finger-pointing ensues.

By focusing on the Bridgestone name and its performance reputation, they can claim their rightful position as one of the big three in the world (Goodyear, Michelin, and Bridgestone). This would give them enormous credentials.

If Bridgestone could get its lesser "stone" off its back, it could focus on a new technology to impress potential tire buyers—something analogous to what Michelin did long ago with radial technology and Goodyear did with Aquatread. One possibility could be low-noise tread design. They could introduce the "Quiet Tire" ("QT" for short). In promoting this new technology, they have a natural visual device: the sound meter. This demonstration will also begin to make people aware of just how noisy their tires can be (also, quietness has come to mean quality in the mind of the consumer).

Credentials first. Technology second. Put those two together and Bridgestone would be on the map in the minds of American tire buyers as a quality tire instead of just the owner of a dying and defective brand called Firestone. They also can better take advantage of their strong OEM position with the Japanese brands and move to replace Firestone's OEM business with Bridgestone tires. The Firestone name can be kept for a while as a value brand (no more racing; no more advertising). They should use their money to build the Bridgestone brand as well as to take advantage of opportunities that could come along (more on this later).

But, as this is being written, Firestone has launched an advertising program to try to restore its badly tarnished reputation. It's time for another lesson.

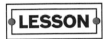 ### Don't try to change the market's mind.

Over the years, I have watched and written about companies who have blown a lot of money trying to change minds in the marketplace.

As mentioned, Xerox and AT&T lost billions trying to convince the market that they could make machines that didn't make a copy or a call.

No one would buy their computers.

Volkswagen dropped over 60 share points, trying to convince the market that VW wasn't just a small, reliable, economical car like the Beetle.

No one bought their big, fast cars.

Coca-Cola blew both prestige and money in an effort to convince the market they had a better thing than the Real Thing.

No one bought their New Coke.

When the market makes up its mind about a product, there's no changing those perceptions.

And now, Firestone is going to try and convince us that we should forget all those thousands of stories about their bad tires. They want to have a "New Beginning."

Firestone's new advertising campaign tells us how well they are now making tires. Unfortunately, right in the middle of the campaign, Ford announced it would replace up to 13 million Firestone tires to the tune of 3 billion dollars. The reason given: "Tires not covered in the original recall could experience increased failure rates." Firestone then fired Ford as a customer and both companies are currently accusing the other in the media. Oops, there goes the relationship and the ad campaign.

Well, maybe Americans will forgive and forget, but my prediction is that no one will buy those tires unless they get a terrific deal on them.

Trying to Change Attitudes

In the book *The Reengineering Revolution* (New York: HarperBusiness, 1995), MIT professor-turned-consultant Michael Hammer calls human beings' innate resistance to change "the most perplexing, annoying, distressing, and confusing part" of reengineering.

To help us better understand this resistance, a book entitled *Attitudes and Persuasion* (Westview Press, 1996) offers some insights. Written by Richard Petty and John Cacioppo, it spends some time on "belief systems." Here's their take on why minds are so hard to change:

> The nature and structure of belief systems is important from the perspective of an informational theorist, because beliefs are enough to provide the cognitive foundation of an attitude. In order to change an attitude, then, it is presumably necessary to modify the information on which that attitude rests. It is generally necessary, therefore, to change a person's beliefs, eliminate old beliefs, or introduce new beliefs.

And you're going to do all that with a 30-second commercial? Not likely.

What Psychologists Say

The Handbook of Social Psychology (Oxford University Press, 1998) reinforces how tough it is to change attitudes.

Any program to change attitudes offers formidable problems. The difficulty of changing a person's basic beliefs, even through so elaborate and intense a procedure as psychotherapy, becomes understandable, as does the fact that procedures that are effective in changing some attitudes have little effect on others.

And what makes things even worse is that truth has no real bearing on these issues. Check out this observation:

> People have attitudes on a staggeringly wide range of issues. They seem to know what they like (and especially dislike) even regarding objects about which they know little, such as Turks, or which have little relevance to their daily concerns, like life in outer space.

So, to paraphrase that old TV show, *Mission Impossible*, if your assignment, Mr. Phelps, is to change people's minds, don't accept the assignment.

It makes more sense for Bridgestone/Firestone to put its money into building the Bridgestone brand as well as into developing new opportunities for the marketplace. Their chances of improving their reputation are nil. This brings us to another lesson.

 **Don't put good money on a dying brand. Put it on a new idea.**

If Bridgestone is to be the performance brand as well as the corporate name, and if Firestone is to be reduced to a value brand with little support, then what do they do with their Dayton brand, which is currently a "value tire"? After all, how many value-price tires do they need?

With all the noise and controversy on tires for the small trucks and SUVs that have flooded the market, there might be an opportunity for a new "specialist" idea in the marketplace. At present, the big tire brands are operating on the everything-for-everybody principle. Their approach is that of being a generalist in tires. Whatever kind of tire you want we've got: high performance, value, passenger car, or truck. Interestingly, specialists tend to win the marketing wars because they can focus on one product, one benefit, and one message. Thus they can become the "expert" or "best" in a category.

A Specialist in Light Truck Tires

Bridgestone would be in a unique position to announce to the world that all the problems they have faced point to the need for a tire that is engineered specifically for the SUV and light truck market—not a brand that is making tires for every kind of vehicle. That brand could be a new one or it could be the Dayton brand repositioned as the specialist in light truck tires. The concept would require a tough name such as:

Dayton Destroyer.
The meanest, toughest
truck tire on the market.

Interestingly, Bridgestone wouldn't have to do a lot of product planning. They already have this type of tire in the Bridgestone truck tire line. They would need only to change the molds to say "Dayton" and then introduce it as a specialist organization that designs tires just for trucks, not passenger cars.

I see no long-term future for Firestone except as a price brand. Bridgestone is the future and should be positioned as one of the world's leading tires. New technology should be developed to support this concept. Either a new brand or the Dayton brand should be positioned as the specialist in light truck tires.

In other words, kill one, push one, and give birth to a new one.

CHAPTER 10

Miller Brewing

A "Miller" Too Far

If number one ranked Anheuser-Busch had been able to pick a number two competitor, they couldn't have done much better than to pick the Miller Brewing Company, which didn't stand a chance. The numbers tell the story.

In 1970, Anheuser-Busch sat on top of the brewing world. They shipped 22,201,811 barrels of beer while the number two, Joseph Schlitz Brewing Company brewed 15,129,000 barrels. About that time, Philip Morris acquired Miller and added a lot of marketing muscle.

Marlboro Meets Miller

A May 1976 *Forbes* article summed up the situation:

> Miller was a sickly company run by an aging management group when Philip Morris acquired it from W. R. Grace in 1969. Its High

Life beer was one of the three truly national premium priced brands, along with Budweiser and Schlitz, yet several regional brewers outsold it in the U.S. market.

Philip Morris's purchasing of Miller, as it turned out, proved the final key to Miller's meteoric rise both as a brand and as a brewery. Philip Morris president George Weissmann waited until late 1971 before installing his own management team of tobacco executives at Miller. Most beer executives and industry experts were unprepared for the full-scale assault Miller was poised to launch to quickly overcome competitors and become a dominant player in the market.

To this end, Weissmann's new team made a conscious decision to employ the same marketing techniques that had spurred the Marlboro Man to fame during the 1960s. For Miller High Life, a venerable but underperforming brand, the problem was one of poor positioning. Their campaign was a model of refinement featuring jazz trumpeter Al Hirt. "Sold for years as the champagne of beers, High Life was," according to a November 8, 1976, *Business Week* article, "attracting a disproportionate share of women and upper-income consumers who were not big beer drinkers. . . . A lot of people drank the beer, but none drank it in quantity."

The solution seemed as simple as selling cigarettes to the heavy cigarette user through a strong brand association. Instead of being held back by the champagne crowd, High Life would now be targeted at blue-collar workers, younger drinkers, and males in general, who together made up the bulk of beer drinkers measured in terms of consumption (Joe six-pack was the target). Advertisements for High Life began featuring young people riding in dune buggies and oil drillers sipping on a cool one after squelching an oil blowout.

Simple yet effective, "Now Comes Miller Time" carried the High Life brand through an enormously profitable decade. In 1975, Miller Brewing posted sales of $658 million and became the fourth-highest beer seller in the country. Two years later, Miller

High Life overtook Schlitz's number two position on the charts. With the financial clout and marketing savvy of Philip Morris backing it, the Miller brand name had by this time truly come into its own.

Let There Be Lite

By 1980, Miller was the second largest brewer in the United States. Anheuser-Busch was on top with 50 million barrels, but Miller had climbed into a strong second place with 37,300,000 barrels sold. The company attained this enviable ranking with the help of the High Life brand. But another, newer product would also be responsible for sustaining the feat. This product was Miller Lite. As early as 1978, William Flanagan, writing for *Esquire,* decreed the now legendary product "by any measure, the most successful in the history of the beer industry." Much later, in 1991, brand and marketing authority David A. Aaker conferred even greater status on Lite lauding it as "one of the most successful new products every introduced" (in the history of advertising). Why was the product so successful? Some might argue that it was inherently unique. Others would say that its introduction was well timed. Still others might contend that it benefited from highly effective advertising. All would probably be correct to some degree.

But to me, this was a case of starting a new category. Miller Lite successfully pioneered the low-calorie beer category on a national basis. And that category is now responsible for well over one-third of all domestic beer sold. (Others had failed where Miller succeeded.)

The first light beer was marketed by the Piels Brewing Company under the name Trommer's Red Letter in 1964, but was taken off the market within weeks of its introduction; the beer had been expressly promoted to women drinkers. Then, in 1967, came a beer by Rheingold named Gablinger's, marketed to men who had a desire for staying slim. Gablinger's also failed. The same year, Peter Hand Brewing of Chicago, makers of Meister Brau, began similarly promoting Meister Brau Lite. The brand survived for five years but was largely unsuccessful.

In June 1972, Miller acquired the Chicago brewer and the Lite trademark, along with several others. Existing market research for Meister Brau Lite, according to Flanagan, "showed a lot more consumer interest in a low-calorie beer than sales had reflected, even among heavy drinkers."

Miller's top management decided to refurbish the brand and then take a page from the High Life campaign to retarget and promote it. With the fitness craze fully underway, they reasoned that the time was ripe as well. After brew masters modified the original recipe and graphic designer Walter Landor—who had made his reputation with several designs for Philip Morris cigarettes—completed his work, Miller Lite was prepared for test-marketing in four cities in mid-1973. The results were so favorable that a national rollout was planned for January 1975, supported by an advertising budget of $12 million (oh, how costs have changed).

Macho Low Calorie

Bob Lenz, creative director at McCann-Erickson, was handed the task of devising a television campaign that would promote the brand to the largest segment of the beer-drinking population while avoiding the potentially negative connotations of the phrases "low-calorie" or "diet" beer. According to Michael Gershman in *Getting It Right the Second Time* (*Marketing Week*, March 25, 1991), when "Lenz saw an ad featuring New York Jets star Matt Snell on a New York bus (he) put 'beer' and 'athletes' together in his mind." The first Lite commercial, starring Snell, was taped in July 1973. Little did anyone realize that the spot would lead to dozens more over a nearly 20-year period, and that its highly touted product would be the catalyst for a proliferation of all types of light foods as well as light beverages.

The "Tastes Great/Less Filling" commercials, which over the years featured the likes of Bob Uecker, Bubba Smith, Dick Butkus,

Wilt Chamberlain, John Madden, Mickey Mantle, Joe Frazier, and nonsports figures Rodney Dangerfield and Mickey Spillane, were resoundingly successful not only because of their celebrity casts, but also because of the wisecracks and comfortable settings (first bars exclusively, later many other sites). The tag line "everything you always wanted in a beer—and less" and the phrase "less filling" were also successful as clever inducements that did not deter from the macho, or at least "regular guy," image the ads were attempting to promote. When Anheuser-Busch unveiled its Natural Light beer, it seemed to borrow heavily from the Lite commercials, and even employed former Lite spokespersons. Lite countered with even funnier sketches that revolved around debates of "Tastes Great/Less Filling" and starred Tommy Heinsohn and referee Mendy Rudolph.

It was a runaway success. In Lite's introductory year, the brand hit $100 million and a production of 12.6 million barrels or approximately 20 percent of Miller's total output. In 1979, Lite surpassed Schlitz in the premium beer rankings; four years later, Lite settled into the number two position behind Budweiser.

Problems Begin

Miller Lite's success spawned a host of competitors, all of which were permitted, despite Miller's best legal efforts, to use the word "Light" for their own brand name for low-calorie beers. This set the stage for a painful lesson for Miller.

 **Generic brand names are never as good as real brand names.**

Miller went "over the edge" with its "Lite" brand name: It was too close to the generic term "light" and became a general name for all products of its class rather than a trade name for a specific product. Lite had the enormous advantage of being the first successful light beer in the mind, yet the name's generic association turned out to be a serious disadvantage. Renamed Miller Lite, the brand currently is a poor second to Bud Light and, down the road, will probably lose out to Coors Light.

But this trouble took a number of years to play out in the market. Before that happened, the bottom started to fall out beneath Miller's flagship brand of High Life.

The Cannibalization of High Life

High Life's reign as the number two beer, which had begun in 1977, was almost over before it started. Production for the aging super brand had already peaked by 1979. By 1985, this number was nearly halved, though High Life had managed to hold the number three slot after being edged aside by its lighter counterpart. That same year, the company reacted to stem the tide by spending $60 million with a new ad agency, J. Walter Thompson, to launch the "Made the American Way" campaign. By 1986, such dire prognostications as Mathew Heller's in *Forbes* were becoming common: "High Life each day looks more like a dying label. And [Thompson's campaign] failed to resuscitate it."

Many observers saw High Life's misfortune as simply the necessary balance to Lite's dramatic rise in prominence. Statistical evidence supports this view. As sales of Miller Lite went from 9.5 percent share of the U.S. beer market in 1978 to 19 percent in 1986, the Miller High Life brand declined from 21 percent to 12 percent in the same period. When you chart the rise of Miller Lite and the decline of Miller's High Life it's almost a perfect "X." It points to another lesson learned the hard way.

 **In the mind, it's one idea to a brand.**

We call this the fish or fowl problem. There's a famous design that portrays fish and fowl in such a way that you cannot see both at the same time. So it is with the human mind. People will see you in only one way. Heinz was once a pickle in the mind. Then they decided to become a ketchup. Today they are the dominant ketchup brand and a fast-disappearing pickle. It's one idea to a brand.

Miller could not be a premium beer and a light beer in the mind at the same time. Very quickly, Miller became a light beer that tasted great but was less filling. It was good night and good luck for Miller High Life. The "champagne of bottled beer" had lost all its bubbles.

In 1991, *Adweek's Marketing Week* (March 25, 1991) bestowed the unwelcome distinction of "dinosaur brand" on Miller High Life and several other well-known but fading products. The editor wrote: "Like the brontosaurus and triceratops of old, these brands have failed the Darwinian selection process, and have probably matured beyond the point where they can ever grow or change again with the times." (He left out that Miller High Life was devoured by a family member.)

One would have thought that this experience would have kept Miller from repeating its mistake. As described earlier in the Xerox case study, marketing people never give up. More Millers entered the fray.

The Miller Children

Miller Genuine Draft, brewed through a cold-filtered process developed by Japan's Sapporo Breweries, was introduced in 1985 and rolled out nationally in 1986. Since that time, it has earned a reputation as the fastest-growing premium beer in the nation. In the words of Patricia Sellers in *Fortune*, Genuine Draft is "the industry's most successful new product since Bud Light came out in 1981"; by the end of 1992 it ranked as the sixth best-selling domestic beer. Its appeal has been primarily to "young, upscale drinkers," a segment that the "Tastes Great" Lite ads had seemed to unconsciously eschew and the High Life ads appeared to lose during the 1980s.

The introductions of Genuine Draft and its cohorts (Miller Reserve and Reserve Light in 1990, and Lite Ultra and Genuine Draft Light in 1991) only repeated history. In 1991, Miller Lite reported its first sales decline ever. What Lite did to High Life, Genuine Draft was doing to Lite. It was dé jà vu all over again.

Lesson learned? No way.

A "Clear" Beer?

Rather than hunker down and get back to basics, the Miller people risked an even more outlandish venture. Early in 1993, Miller Brewing began test-marketing Miller Clear. That's right, a beer with no amber color. They took a traditionally brewed beer through a "special ultra-filtration process that delivers a distinctive taste and makes the beer clear." It looked like a bottle of water or maybe a bottle of what they used to wash out the vats. Who knows what it was?

But it was a dismal failure. Any beer that didn't look like beer was never going to taste very good. (The same fate befell Pepsi Crystal, the first clear cola.) "The idea of clear beer never made any real sense," said beverage consultant Tom Pirko, president of Bevmark Inc. in New York. "As far as consumers are concerned, clearness is for a few basic reasons: The product is pure, natural, or more stylish. Beyond that there aren't too many good reasons."

Pirko added that as a fashion trend clearness was a bold statement, but fashions come and go.

You would think that dumb idea and the millions it cost would have finally ended it all. Lesson learned? No way.

Just Plain "Miller"

The boys at Miller had one last big idea to put into the market. In early 1996, they launched what they hoped would be their premium priced flagship brand. Their Budweiser so to speak. This was needed since their last premium priced flagship, High Life, was now sold on price.

So they launched Miller Beer. The rationale for naming the beer simply "Miller" was explained with the line: "We're just calling it who we are." Well, that might be true but since they had been around for so long pushing the Miller name on so many products, most people didn't even realize it was a new beer.

Despite a $50 million launch and the diversion of funds from the Red Dog and Miller Genuine Draft brands, just plain Miller never went anywhere. A parade of agencies came up with a parade of different ideas. There were flavor ideas, there were raunchy humor ideas, there were Generation Xers ideas such as "It's not my brand but it's good."

That didn't aptly sell any beer but it described the problem. It became no one's brand and it is no longer with us.

From Challenger to Also-Ran

In 20 years of endless introductions of Miller this, Miller that, or just plain Miller, the brand has made very little progress. Where they were once a close second, only 12 million barrels behind Anheuser-Busch, today they are a distant second with Anheuser outselling them by 45 million barrels or so. Since the spread is more than Miller sells, you can say they've been lapped.

Sales and share continue to decline, management has come and gone, agencies have come and gone, yet no one has been able to improve things. What's in play here is a very important lesson.

 **A brand that's many things can't be one thing.**

What started out in 1978 as a classic pilsner has become a portfolio of beers. Each brand in the portfolio suffers from a bad case of line extension. If you want a Miller beer, the next question will be "Which one?" Do you want Miller Lite, Miller Lite Ice, Miller

Genuine Draft, Miller Genuine Draft Lite, Miller High Life, Miller High Life Lite, or Miller High Life Ice?"

Oh forget it, I'll have a Budweiser.

They also own the Jacob Leinenkugel Brewing Company. It has the same problem—you have to figure out whether you want a Leinenkugel's Original Premium, Leinenkugel's Light, Leinenkugel's Northwoods Lager, Leinenkugel's Genuine Bock (seasonal), Leinenkugel's Red Lager, Leinenkugel's Honey Weiss, Leinenkugel's Berry Weiss (seasonal), Leinenkugel's Hefeweizen (draft only), or Leinenkugel's Creamy Dark.

Oh forget it, I'll have a Budweiser.

And to compound the problem, they've just acquired Henry Weinhard, which comes in these flavors: Private Reserve, Dark, Porter, Amber Ale, Pale Ale, Hazelnut Stout, Blackberry Wheat, Hefeweizen, and Red Lager.

Oh forget it, I'll have a Budweiser.

They also have a Red Dog, an Icehouse, and Southpaw Light. Or Old English 800 Malt Liquor, Old English 800 Ice, and Old English 800 Mixed Fruit.

Oh forget it, I'm going home.

It's no wonder that agencies can't figure out how to advertise these brands, wholesalers continue to express their discontent, and Philip Morris wants to sell the business. It's like trying to market a person with multiple personalities. Which one do you pick to promote? It's an impossible problem.

Line Extension Redux

At the heart of this problem is our old nemesis, line extension; nothing else has caused as much trouble. Let's review the bidding.

In *Positioning: The Battle for Your Mind* (McGraw-Hill, 1980), there are two chapters on the problems of line extension.

In *The 22 Immutable Laws of Marketing* (HarperCollins, 1993), it became the single most violated law.

In *The New Positioning* (McGraw-Hill, 1995), I wrote about the problem as a "Matter of Perspective":

> The difference in views on this subject is essentially a perspective. Companies look at their brands from an economic point of view. To gain cost efficiencies and trade acceptance, they are quite willing to turn a highly focused brand, one that stands for a certain type of product or idea, into an unfocused brand that represents two or three or more types of products or ideas. We look at the issue of line extension from the point of view of the mind. The more variations you attach to the brand, the more the mind loses focus. Gradually, a brand like Chevrolet comes to mean nothing at all.

Still in the Wilderness

My lack of approval has not slowed anyone down. In fact, quite the opposite has been true. "Extending brand equity" has become all the rage, as marketing experts and consultants talk about concepts such as "megabrands."

For years, we were the lonely voices railing against line extension. Even the *Journal of Consumer Marketing* noticed this: "Ries and Trout stand alone as the only outright critics of the practice of brand extension."

Neither has support from the *Harvard Business Review* (November–December, 1994) slowed down the line extension express. And their verdict was severe: "Unchecked product-line expansion can weaken a brand's image, disturb trade relations, and disguise cost increases."

Nowhere has this damage been as visible as in the beer business. Miller has all but destroyed what Miller means. Budweiser has too many "Buds for you," and Bud Light is eating into basic Budweiser. Coors Light has pretty much done in Regular Coors.

And they wonder why the beer business has been flat all these years. With so much confusion, it has become, "Oh forget it, I'll have a bottle of water."

11

Marks & Spencer

A Bad Case of "Top-Down" Thinking

Marks & Spencer is the United Kingdom's leading clothing retailer. But they have begun to fall from their lofty perch on top of the retail world. Their problem is a bad case of ignoring change, which can be a deadly mistake.

In 1993, Al Ries, my ex-partner, and I wrote about change in *The 22 Immutable Laws of Marketing* (HarperBusiness, 1993). It was described in what we called the "Law of Division." This law makes the point that, over time, a category will divide and become two or more categories. Like an amoeba dividing in a petri dish, the marketing arena supports an ever-expanding sea of categories. It's why you have to be aware of the changes that are always underway.

A category starts off as a single entity such as computers. But over time, the category breaks up into other segments: Mainframes, minicomputers, workstations, personal computers, laptops, notebooks, pen computers.

Beer started the same way. Today we have imported and domestic beer; premium and popular priced beers; light, draft, ice, and dry beers. (Clear, as mentioned, never made it as a category but nonalcoholic did.)

The Cause of Problems

Each market segment is a separate, distinct entity. And each segment has its own leader, which is rarely the same leader of the original category. IBM is the leader in mainframes, Sun in workstations, Compaq in PCs, and so on.

Instead of understanding the concept of division, many corporate leaders hold the naive belief that because they are a big deal in the original category they can be a big deal in the emerging new segments of the business. They try to take a well-known brand name in one category and use the same brand name in a new category.

Another problem is that instead of understanding this concept of division, many corporate leaders hold the belief that categories are combining. Words like synergy, corporate alliance, and convergence are buzzwords in boardrooms all around the world. The merger of AOL and Time Warner was based on the convergence of different forms of media (computer, television, and print). Good luck, it won't happen. Categories are dividing, not combining. And the way for a leader to maintain its dominance is to address each emerging category with a different brand name, as General Motors did in the early days.

So it is in the retail world, which has exploded with specialty retailers, discount retailers, and you-name-it retailers. The sad saga of the United Kingdom's famous ailing retailer, Marks & Spencer, describes a company that failed to understand the law of division.

A Long Heritage

Michael Marks, a Russian refugee, hired an open stall in the Kirk-gate market in Leeds. Marks then formed a partnership with Tom Spencer, a cashier in a wholesale company. The company then embarked on a number of bold moves. In 1920, they bought manufacturing companies. They introduced a food department in 1931. They opened stores in Paris and Brussels in 1973. In 1986, they started selling furniture. In 1988, they went to the United States and acquired Brooks Brothers and Kings Supermarkets. Then it was off to the Far East to open new stores. While all this looked good on the surface, behind all the activity and press releases was a company in deep trouble. Its core business was going bad.

Trouble Appears

In 1998, Marks & Spencer's earnings took a dramatic tumble. The biggest problems were in Marks & Spencer's U.K. retailing area, but their foreign operations were also going sour. The grand international expansion strategy was in tatters.

Suddenly there was a boardroom battle and their long-serving CEO, Richard Greenbury, was in the crosshairs. What became apparent was a bad case of ignoring change as the market segmented.

As losses continued in 1999, Greenbury retired and the CEO title went to Peter Salsbury, also a homegrown manager. As the stock plummeted and nothing got better, he was also under pressure.

Change Ignored

During the 1990s, a revolution was going on in U.K. retailing, particularly in increased customer service and in the nature and strength of the competition.

Marks & Spencer's failure to notice these changes has been laid at the feet of the aforementioned Richard Greenbury, who was appointed chief executive in 1988. He had been with Marks & Spencer all his working life, rising to the top of the company and becoming chairman as well in 1991. The key to his strategy for M&S was cost control, by keeping employee numbers to a minimum (the "staring at your navel" strategy).

However, by the mid-1990s, customers' expectations were rising and other stores were responding with higher and increasingly innovative levels of service. These could not be matched by Marks & Spencer where too few sales assistants resulted in poorer services and unhappy customers. Internal Marks & Spencer documents show that only 62 percent of M&S customers graded its service "good" in March 1998, compared with 71 percent in November 1995. Furthermore, the proportion of customers who regarded Marks & Spencer as "value for money" had dropped from 69 percent in 1995 to 57 percent in March 1998. These problems were shielded from Greenbury, who was noted for being difficult and unapproachable. On his frequent store visits, extra staff were brought in to give the illusion of good service, and he claims that he never received the customer survey results.

 Don't expect your people to bring you the bad news.

Survival is built into human nature. And any good manager with a PowerPoint presentation knows better than to tell the CEO that the company is in trouble. The manager realizes that on hearing this news, the CEO will instantly launch a search for those responsible for the problems (the "off with their heads" reaction). And the person making the presentation, who probably has some form of involvement, could be in considerable trouble. Better to keep the bad news hidden or at least camouflaged within some good news.

Consider what happened at Lucent when their financial officer, Patricia Russo, told the then CEO, Rich McGinn, that the numbers he was feeding Wall Street were bad. In no time at all, she was toast. Of course, after her dismissal, it turned out she was right and it was McGinn's turn to become toast. But most stories like this don't have a happy ending where truth wins out and the bad guys are dismissed. More times than not, people think truth is something to avoid if you want to keep your job.

A good leader must find out for himself or herself what is really going on. You can't remain isolated in your office. Mr. Greenbury was not in touch with the rapid changes occurring in the marketplace and his autocratic style made it hard for his managers to communicate with him.

Sam Walton kept in touch by driving his pickup truck down to the Wal-Mart loading docks and chatting with the boys about what was happening.

Jack Welch spent a lot of time at GE's training facility talking with the up-and-coming managers of his far-flung empire. Welch encouraged no-holds-barred discussions about the state of GE.

Beware of the bureaucracy, they might not tell you the truth.

Problems Abound

Back at Marks & Spencer there was plenty of bad news to consider. The younger generation had dramatically shifted to buying more exciting branded goods from other stores. Shoppers in their 30s and 40s used to dress like their parents. Now many of them wanted to dress like their kids. And it has been a long time since any self-respecting teenager went willingly to a Marks & Spencer store to buy clothes.

One reason was that the store layout looked like a hangover from a bygone era, especially when compared with the jazzy store layouts of rivals such as Gap and Next. This was compounded by some bad decisions in 1998 featuring acres of gray and black clothing that made the store layouts look even worse.

Behind this decline were two basic faults. The first was a rigid top-down "head office knows best" culture built on their record of success. This was fine only so long as customers kept coming and the competition lagged behind. This led to outmoded rules that meant the staff spent too much time on rituals such as checking stock or counting cash in the tills because that was the way it had always been done.

Add to this an inbred management with few appointments from outside the company and you can see why things at Marks & Spencer never changed in a changing world.

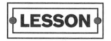 **Good management is a "bottom-up" process.**

The problems of Marks & Spencer were that of a classic top-down management system. Over the years, an enormous amount of trouble has been caused by top management obsessed with "what they want to do." What are long-term plans except a meticulous outline of where managers want their company to be in 5 years or 10 years?

- Managers who plan from the top down are trying to force things to happen. Managers who plan from the bottom are trying to find things to exploit.

- Top-down managers chase existing markets. Bottom-up managers look for new opportunities.

- Top-down managers are internally oriented. Bottom-up mangers are externally oriented.

- Top-down managers believe in long-term success and short-term losses. Bottom-up managers believe in short-term success and long-term success.

We've written extensively about this subject in our book *Bottom-Up Marketing* (McGraw-Hill, 1989). The following sections briefly reprise the key steps in the bottom-up process, none of which were in play at Marks & Spencer.

Going Down to the Front

To figure out what to do, you must leave your ivory tower and go down to the front where the marketing battle is being fought. Don't confuse going down to the front with sending someone down to the front. In most companies, a lot of sending goes on. There's personal sending, as in asking for reports from the sales force. There's also impersonal sending, as in commissioning a marketing research study.

There's nothing wrong with marketing research as long as you remember that marketing is a game of the future. Most marketing research is a report on the past. Research tells you what prospects have already done, not necessarily what they are going to do. (Marketers don't know what prospects are going to do, so don't confuse them by asking.)

There's nothing wrong with sending someone to the front either. But nothing is better than getting your information first-hand. Too many managers think they can run a marketing operation from an office. "A desk," wrote novelist John Le Carré, "is a dangerous place from which to watch the world."

Where Is the Front?

The front line of a marketing war is not where you might expect to find it.

It's not the department store, the drugstore, or the customer's office. The front line is the mind of the prospect. Going down to the front means putting yourself in a position to explore what customers and prospects might be thinking. (To become a good fisherman, you have to think like a fish.)

In the motion picture *Big*, Tom Hanks has the body of a man but the mind of a 13-year-old kid. Naturally, a toy company CEO instantly makes Tom a vice president.

The front can be in your own home, watching a spouse decide which brand to buy or not to buy. Ask why he or she decided to buy a particular brand of toothpaste or shampoo. And don't confine your questions to just your own product category. A good marketing person has a feel for a variety of marketing battles, not just his or her own.

If you don't explore a variety of marketing battles, you tend to get the feeling that everybody in the world spends his or her time evaluating the brands in your product category.

Chief Executives Tend to Lose Touch

The bigger the company, the more likely it is that the chief executive has lost touch with the front lines. This might be the single most important factor limiting the success of a corporation. Because of the time required to run a large organization, chief executives delegate the marketing function.

How should a CEO operate? Andrew S. Grove of Intel said it best: "There's a tendency at the senior and middle-manager levels to be too big-picturish and too superficial. One can formulate brilliant global strategies whose executability is zero. It's only through familiarity with details—the capability of the individuals who have to execute, the marketplace, the timing—that a good strategy emerges."

Grove sums up his approach in one sentence: "I like to work up from details to big pictures."

This is the essence of *bottom-up marketing*.

The Problems of the CEO

If you're the chief executive officer, you have a big advantage in the development of strategy: You can approve the program and it gets implemented. The CEO, however, is often the person most out of touch with the marketplace. (You don't get to be CEO by pleasing the customer. You get to be CEO by pleasing the previous CEO, who is usually even more out of touch than you are.)

One problem is the number of management layers between the top and the bottom. The more layers, the more you are insulated from the market. The rich white frosting at the top of many corporations is increasingly divorced from the soggy realities at the bottom of the cake. The layers tend to filter out the bad news and pass along only the good news. When things start to go bad, the CEO is often the last to know.

Reducing the number of layers is one way for a chief executive to get psychologically closer to the front. One study of 60 companies showed that the top performers had less than four management layers; poor ones had about eight. The number of layers in a large organization makes it difficult for a chief executive to go down to the front. Lower-level people turn most visits to the battleground into a ceremonial "Grand Tour." Everything is cleaned up and carefully orchestrated to look good. You are encouraged to think of your visit as a morale-building trip, not as an information-gathering venture. "Blow a little sunshine into the trenches," says the tour guide.

Monitoring the Trends

To make sure your strategy is in tune with the future, you have to be aware of the trends taking place in your category. It's only a fad if it's fast moving.

When you begin to monitor the trends, keep in mind that most of the trends are manufactured to sell newspapers or magazines, not to help you market your products. Yet marketing people tend to believe the hype rather than the reality. "The consumer marketing equation continues to change in profound and irreversible ways," said one management guru. "So a basic change in attitude is needed: from managing businesses to managing change."

Where are all those changes? What happened to the paperless, cashless, checkless society?

What happened to the Third Wave, Megatrend, Second Industrial Revolution, Information-Oriented Society where everyone works at home in front of a computer/picture phone terminal?

As a matter of fact, what happened to the picture phone?

Did you get your helicopter yet? Where is the marvelous device that was going to replace your car and make the superhighway obsolete?

Have you been getting your electronic newspaper delivered daily through your television set as promised three decades ago?

The reality never seems to catch up with the hype. The future always seems to be just over the next hill.

You Can't Predict the Enemy

Generals who make military plans based on "knowing" what the enemy is going to do are "predicting the enemy," which is another way of predicting the future. They usually turn out to be losing generals. Winning generals tend to make military plans that are workable regardless of the enemy's movement. This is the essence of good strategy.

When you predict what the enemy is going to do, you are buying a lottery ticket with your company's future at stake. Gambling may be all right in Las Vegas, in Atlantic City, or on Wall Street. But it's not good enough for marketing.

The Role of Research

Most of the numbers you need to develop an effective marketing plan can be obtained from your local library, the U.S. government, or your favorite trade publication. This is research that tells you what people have actually done.

When you use research to try to find out what people will do, you run into problems. People often respond to questions in a way they deem is the most socially acceptable. This is especially true in focus groups where other people are looking on behind the one-way mirrors.

The trick is to find a way to get the answers that people keep in the closet. Who wants to admit they eat fast food instead of nutritious food? How many business executives will admit they hate to write letters or find personal computers intimidating? Who will admit to overusing the telephone?

Finding Your Idea

A differentiating idea is what you're after. The best idea is the one that strikes at the weak point of your competitors in the mind of your prospect.

You can go down to the front and monitor the trends only for so long. Sooner or later, you'll have to select a differentiating idea to develop into a strategy. Actually, you might think through the process several times: Choose one idea and carry it to a logical conclusion; then set aside that idea and try another.

There are some principles to keep in mind.

Your Idea Should Not Be Company-Oriented

This is top-down marketing at its worst—selecting an idea because it meets the in-house needs of the corporation.

Xerox bought a computer company (Scientific Data Systems) because it fitted their strategic plans to offer their customers an automated office. It was a billion-dollar mistake. Customers already had a plethora of computer companies from which to choose.

Nine out of ten new products are introduced to fill a void in the company's line, not to fill a void in the marketplace. Maybe that's why nine out of ten new products are also failures.

A company focus is wrong. It might win you Brownie points inside the organization, but it can cause disastrous results on the outside.

Your Idea Should Be Competitor-Oriented

Many years ago, Delta decided to offer a "triple-mileage" bonus to members (and new members) of its frequent flier club. It seemed like a good idea, bound to attract a lot of new business for Delta. It did, but the new program also attracted American, United, Pan Am, TWA, and Eastern. In fact, all of Delta's competitors jumped in and offered the same bonus deal. Nobody benefited except the frequent flier.

When Burger King launched its "broiling, not frying" campaign, McDonald's didn't rip out all the fryers in its restaurants and put in broilers. It would have been enormously expensive to do so.

Triple mileage is not a competitor-oriented strategy because it can be quickly copied. Speed is an important consideration. If a competitor cannot copy your idea quickly, then you have the time to take ownership of the idea in the customer's mind. Most airline passengers don't know that Delta pioneered the triple mileage idea. Delta didn't have enough time to establish the concept before the competition moved in.

"Broiling, not frying" is a good competitor-oriented tactic because it cannot be copied quickly. Nor can it be copied economically.

When Michelin attacked the U.S. market with the radial-ply tire, it put Goodyear and Firestone on the defensive for many years. Even if the big wheels in the U.S. tire industry were willing to invest the money in radial-tire facilities, it would take years to get their production lines running.

The only strategy worth considering is the move that puts the knife into the competition. Moves that just offer the customer some incentive to purchase also offer the competition some incentive to copy. Yet most marketing programs involve coupons, rebates, in-store promotions, and a variety of deals. The ones that don't work cost you money. The ones that do work buy you the sincerest form of flattery; your competitors copy you.

You can't win by pleasing the consumer. Forget the deals. What would please the consumer most is your giving the product away. On the other hand, a strategy that displeases one or more of your competitors is bound to be good for your business.

A Troubled Future?

Last year, Marks & Spencer brought in another face to turn things around. His name is Luc Vandevelde (you're right, he isn't a Brit, he's Belgian) and he wants to turn Marks & Spencer into a great global retailer. And has he got plans.

On the Internet, he wants to create a Marks & Spencer branded community centered round the group's products: Buy one of its safari jackets and Marks & Spencer will offer you a holiday booking.

Offline, he wants to extend the brand into financial services by offering travel insurance. Also there is talk of licensing its expertise in supply chain management.

But mostly, he wants to make international deals that go beyond just a few stores here and there. Already the warning flags are flying. Here's what the *Economist* (October 28, 2000) thinks of all these grand plans:

> The risk is that his plans for M&S reflect frustrated ambition. Does M&S need the international expansion? The past two years have brought enormous turmoil, including falling profits, a boardroom row, job losses and rumors of a takeover. Mr. Salsbury, who was appointed only a year ago, has set about his own changes, including giving shop staff greater control over purchasing, a new look for the stores, de-emphasizing the St. Michael brand, and introducing new designer clothes. All of this is an attempt to switch M&S from a tendency to "push" products that it thinks customers want, instead of being guided by what customers actually buy.
>
> What M&S needs now is time to see if its new ranges have appeal. The group's main task should be to rebuild its tattered franchise in its British heartland. Even if Mr. Vandevelde thinks that

M&S's British problems will be solved, now is not the moment to go on a buying spree. Mr. Vandevelde's dearest wish may be to run a global retailer, but M&S might not be the right vehicle for his ambition.

The *Economist* has a very good point and sets up another important lesson that Marks & Spencer should heed.

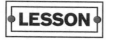 **Too much change can be dangerous.**

When a brand has a long heritage and a loyal following, one runs a big risk with too much change. Nothing demonstrated this better than Coca-Cola's attempt to move to New Coke. Their loyal drinkers were outraged and it took but a matter of weeks for Coke Classic to return and New Coke to begin its exit.

Already, Mr. Vandevelde has launched the first Marks & Spencer advertising campaign. They are resizing clothes to better-fit modern body shapes. They are developing new look "concept" stores and changing store layouts with more coordinated displays and emphasis on "lifestyle."

But changing an image is difficult and dangerous. Some customers like it, others find it confusing; and trust, once lost, is hard to regain. Once you give up what you were, you run the risk of becoming nothing. With too much change, you are telling your loyal customers that they weren't shopping in a very good store. Thus people feel betrayed and alienated. Result: they find another store.

Marks & Spencer is still the largest U.K. clothes retailer, but its market share in clothing has fallen from 16 percent in 1997 to less than 14 percent. From boasting that it could cater to customers from all walks of life, it now says it is firmly focused on the middle market. That market, however, is no longer homogeneous but segmented, with middle-market customers demanding basic items such as T-shirts for everything from gardening to evenings out. The challenge is to provide products for all segments at the best prices without sacrificing quality. But can they do it with one brand name instead of multiple retail brands? (Remember, each emerging segment has its own leader.)

There are no easy answers here. Some of Marks & Spencer's business has gone to other retailers, and they won't get it back unless someone else stumbles. And, at present, they have fierce, fleet-of-foot competition such as Next, Gap, and Top Shop, as well as Tesco in the food category. None of these shows signs of faltering. They also have to deal with overexpansion and too many underperforming stores. They have low staff morale, disillusioned customers, and a declining loyalty to the brand.

My guess is that their future will continue to be very difficult.

CHAPTER 12

Trouble in the Wind

Brands with Unresolved Problems

While you couldn't yet call it big trouble, some brands out there face imminent trouble. And they must make some difficult decisions to pave the way for an untroubled future.

In all cases, they are brands that have to better understand just what issues they must resolve. That lack of awareness is often at the heart of most strategic problems. The crux of the matter is not having a clear focus on just what threatens a brand's long-term health. To this day, General Motors does not seem to recognize that by making their cars look alike and pricing them alike they seriously damaged their five brands. To this day, Miller Beer probably won't acknowledge that line extension was at the heart of their problems. And I know that AT&T never realized the critical need to demonstrate why they were technologically superior to their me-too competitors.

The following brands also face the problem of clearly recognizing what's in the way of their long-term success.

Kellogg's: A Bad Case of Generics

To call Kellogg's Corn Flakes one of the first American health foods is not an exaggeration. In 1898, the Kellogg brothers developed a flaked cereal by running toasted corn mush through metal rollers. The recipe for Corn Flakes has remained unchanged since W.K. Kellogg transformed the product from a private label health food to a mass-marketed breakfast staple.

Corn Flakes remained the best-selling cereal in the United States throughout the first half of the past century. From the mid-1960s on, Kellogg's had at least 40 percent of the market as Corn Flakes was joined by Frosted Flakes, Rice Krispies, Raisin Bran, Froot Loops, Special K, and several lesser brands. But gradually, Kellogg's leadership position has slipped.

No Longer the King

At the end of the 1990s, Kellogg's lost its crown as king of the cereal business to rival General Mills. Not only did sales start to decline but also Cheerios became America's favorite cereal. With this, things hit the fan in Battle Creek, Michigan. Out came the announcement that you usually hear when trouble strikes: *Kellogg's announced a restructuring and a planned reinvestment behind its core products as well as a $4.2 billion deal to acquire the Keebler Foods Company.*

Wall Street was indeed a problem here (more on this in Chapter 15) but what I sense is that Carlos Gutierrez, president and CEO, doesn't yet see the underlying trouble facing Kellogg's.

The Generic Name Problem

What Kellogg's has to deal with is the "Miller Lite problem" to a far greater degree: Corn Flakes, Raisin Bran, and Rice Krispies have become generic. The lesson management really hasn't faced is that *generic brand names are never as good as coined real names*. Their main competitor has real brand names in "Cheerios" and "Wheaties." And Kellogg's most successful brand also has a real brand name: "Frosted Flakes" (as well as Tony the Tiger). Kellogg's is somewhat aware of the problem, as underneath the words Corn Flakes, you'll find "The Original & Best." Nice start, but why are they "the best"?

What is missing here is a program to tell prospective customers why Kellogg's is better than all those other companies pushing the same generic cereals, often at lower prices. The "Best to you each morning" desperately needs the reason why it's so good. Absent that, Cheerios or the cheaper versions of the generics will win the battle. That was the problem one of Kellogg's marketing executives undertook to solve for the Kellogg business in South America where private label generics were a big problem because of lower incomes in the region. In working with him, it became apparent to me that he was on to something that could establish the difference for the Kellogg's brand.

Real versus Processed Cereal

The executive produced a videotape that laid out a strategy to move the Kellogg's name from meaning nothing to meaning a great deal. It was one of the best strategic presentations I have ever seen. Entitled "Real Cereal," it laid out the following strategic points. As with the Burger King analysis, it shows how to construct a simple but powerful step-by-step strategy that pulls no punches while offering a solution:

Real Cereal
- Kellogg's as a brand stands for very little beyond being a manufacturer of cereal. Many don't even know that Kellogg's makes Frosted Flakes.
- Kellogg's invented healthy dry cereal in 1906 with its proprietary manufacturing process using the heart of the corn and adding vitamins.

- Kellogg's was the leader, the original maker of superior grain-based products. The success of these products attracted a lot of me-too, extruded, cheaper products that were not as nutritious or as well fortified.

- Many of these products were aimed at children. The selling points were taste, fun, and promotions. The market became a cartoon battleground.

- Kellogg's moved to cartoons and extruded products. They raised prices and were criticized for having too much sugar, artificial colors, and flavors. Private label products began to take market share. Kellogg's lost share in 20 out of 28 markets around the world. The brand had lost superiority.

- The only strategy open to Kellogg's was to reposition the competition as having processed cereal that is ground up and molded with a spray gun. They should emulate the approach of the Boar's Head brand meats that effectively used a similar real turkey versus ground-up processed turkey strategy. (They ran the Boar's Head commercial at this point.)

- Kellogg's unique but expensive milling process uses whole grain and takes 8 hours versus 8 minutes to make. It also adds more fortification than many of the cheaper, extruded products. Kellogg's Corn Flakes is real cereal. Other cereals (including Cheerios) are processed. Those cereals made by Kellogg's that are processed (such as Froot Loops) should drop the Kellogg's name. It won't be missed.

This approach, if implemented, would tell the dramatic and little known story that explains why the Kellogg's brand is indeed the best for you each morning.

The Future?

That videotape presentation was produced in 1996. While some of that strategy was implemented with some success in South American markets, the U.S. management team never adopted it. They appear to have chosen to put their efforts and money behind the individual brands instead of the Kellogg's brand. This shows me that they don't see or understand the depth of the generic brands problem that is slowly eating into their market share.

And then there's the issue of those little elves at Keebler. How will top management handle this acquisition? Will they try to "run things better"? Will this problem take up a great deal of their corporate energy and resources? The *Delaney Report* (November 20, 2000), an advertising industry newsletter, had this to say about the new CEO, Mr. Gutierrez:

> Carlos grew up in the Kellogg environment. He doesn't have the external exposure to understand how to run things differently. He's all about the Kellogg way of doing things, which is methodical and conservative by nature. More tactical and often times not very strategic.

Things are likely to stay soggy for America's number two cereal maker.

Volvo: Driving the Wrong Way

Volvo entered the U.S. market in 1956 to less than a rousing reception. It was a styling disaster reminiscent of the 1940s. They overcame this by developing a positioning strategy around the car's durability. The concept: *The car built tough enough for the rugged Scandinavian weather and road conditions.*

The ruggedness engineered into Volvo meant that because they lasted longer than the stylish American-made cars, the vehicles were less expensive in the long run. (An early model, the split-grille 1965 Volvo PIZZS had rolled up more than 400,000 miles.) Slowly, a Volvo following began to be developed in the United States.

From Ruggedness to Safety

Out of ruggedness evolved the simple but believable claim that Volvos were safer vehicles to drive. It was reinforced by the fact that the Volvo 144 and the luxury model 164 met all proposed U.S. safety standards of the 1970s even before they were announced. The Volvos had front-seat belts, four-wheel drive, disc brakes, split steering columns, and energy-absorbing front ends. In 1976, the National Highway Traffic Safety Administration used the Volvo 240 as the benchmark for automobile safety in the United States.

In 1982, Volvo introduced the 760, the first of the newly designed 700 series that would become a favorite family car for the "Yuppie" set in the 1980s. In 1985, Volvo became the best-selling European import.

The Bear Foot Blunder

Everything was going swimmingly until 1990 when the infamous commercial ran that featured a 10,000-pound monster truck called Bear Foot driving over a Volvo roof with no apparent damage. While the commercial was based on an actual event, this time the roof was reinforced with wooden and steel framing, and the Texas Attorney General's office busted Volvo for misleading and deceptive advertising.

The resulting controversy cost the New York ad agency, Scali, McCabe its 23-year-old account and certainly didn't boost the believability of the tagline, "A car you can believe in."

Drive Safely

The new agency introduced the brilliant tagline: Drive Safely, and they reinforced this with ads about daytime running lights and side impact air bags. Volvo said the slogan grew from the realization that "Volvo is safety." But instead of pursuing this strategy, Volvo slowly started to develop an everything-for-everybody strategy. They ignored the lesson that *focus is critical in a competitive world.*

In 1991, Volvo unveiled the 850 GLT, a sports sedan that the company hoped would broaden its appeal to younger and older drivers without children. Volvo promoted the 850 as a fun car to drive but found it difficult to overcome its own carefully crafted car reputation. The *New York Times* reviewed the car in such a way that Volvo probably received the wrong message: "Volvo has wrapped its big news in the same square lines that has typified the Swedish maker's body armor for the past quarter century."

The End of the Boxy Look?

The review and the 850's lack of success may have led Volvo to think that the key to not selling a lot of 850s was its traditional tanklike styling. The word probably went out to the design department to start thinking about a design that looked sleek and fast instead of safe.

What Volvo is less likely to have realized is that what the *New York Times* called "body armor" styling is one of the biggest factors in the perception of its being a safe car. Just as a Ferrari's sleek styling reinforces its perception of being fast (even parked, it looks dangerous), the Volvo's tankish shape helps convince people of its safety.

Although moving away from the boxy look will undermine Volvo's uniqueness, this is exactly what they appear to be doing. They have come out with a convertible, which is not a very safe idea, and stylish coupes that sure don't look like tanks.

A Volvo executive expressed the company's need to change this way, "There are too many people who think they aren't allowed to buy a Volvo unless they are married and have two kids under 12." Well, that may be so, but when you consider that a baby is born every 8 seconds in the United States, it's a market that isn't going to dwindle away very soon.

If Volvo continues down this everything-for-everybody road, one can only look out for a car wreck in the not too distant future.

Kodak: Struggling in a Changing World

Like AT&T, General Motors, and IBM, Kodak is an industry icon that is having difficulty dealing with competition and new technology. Because of their long history of success, they have put inordinate faith in their name and logo. They could do what they wanted to do.

A fundamental mistake that big successful companies often make is to see themselves and their reputation far beyond the way the world is willing to see them. The corporate feeling is, "All I have to do is put my well-known name on the product and the world will buy it."

No they won't. Especially if you're horning in on someone else's specialty. And besides, the world also loves an alternative. So if you're sitting there all alone, enjoy it while you can for as soon as an attractive alternative comes along, you're going to lose some business.

Where Simple Picture Taking Began

During the 1870s, George Eastman, a young bank clerk in Rochester, New York, took an avid interest in photography. But wet-plate photographic equipment was bulky and unwieldy, so people could not take a camera on a trip. A photographer traveled with the photographic outfit of which the camera was only a part. After much work in his mother's sink, Eastman came up with dry plates and gelatin-coated paper "film" to be used with his new patented roll holder. Small cameras were then possible, and at last, people could take easy-to-use cameras everywhere.

The brand name, Kodak, was another invention of Eastman. "K" happened to be his favorite letter. He also liked the name because it was short, easily pronounced, and didn't resemble any other brand name in the industry. It was and is a brilliant name.

He topped that great name with a brilliant positioning line for his advertising:

Kodak Cameras.
You press the button.
We do the rest.

The rest is history: Photography became a gigantic industry and that little yellow film box was its visual symbol. Everything went swimmingly until, you guessed it, a strong alternative arrived.

The Little Green Box

In the late 1970s, the weak Japanese yen allowed a very strong competitor to get a toehold in the U.S. market. Fuji Photo entered the fray with a little green box of film that challenged Kodak's dominance in the photographic paper market. By offering a similar quality product at a much lower price, Fuji began capturing a substantial share of the U.S. market through the 1980s and 1990s. In 1996, Kodak had an 80 percent share against Fuji's 10 percent. By the year 2000, Kodak's share was estimated at 65 percent as against Fuji's 25 percent.

The lesson Kodak missed here was that *leaders have to block.* It took too long for Kodak to aggressively reduce its cost and prices to challenge Fuji's aggressive pricing moves. The competitive rule in play is that you always have to stay in the ballpark on pricing. Even the vaunted Marlboro brand discovered this as they dramatically dumped their price to counter the low-price cigarettes. (They dumped their stock price as well.)

By hanging back and allowing a big price differential, Kodak encouraged people to discover that Fuji pictures came out about as well as Kodak pictures. And when in 1984, Kodak lost the title of "official film of the 1984 Summer Olympics" to Fuji, it solidified the perception of its being a legitimate alternative and not just a low-price brand.

Green was here to stay as the alternative to yellow.

The Digital Age

Having to cope with Fuji was one thing but having to cope with the arrival of digital pictures just might be Kodak's ultimate test of survival. To succeed in their next century of existence, they will likely have to shift toward newer digital imaging technologies that will be a far cry from Mother Eastman's sink. Kodak faces fierce competition from U.S. and Japanese companies like Hewlett-Packard, Sony, and Canon that are accustomed to the quick pace of change in digital technology. Many hold that Kodak's chances of making a profit with digital camera manufacturing are slim. Most analysts feel that Kodak will ultimately fail to reinvent itself and make it into the ranks of leading U.S. digital corporations.

I agree with that, especially if you're talking about the brand, "Kodak."

Needed: A New Name

As stated earlier: *If you're known for one thing, the market will not give you another thing.* Kodak is "film" in the minds of the marketplace and not "camera." Nikon, which is a camera in the mind, has a better chance at becoming a successful digital camera (it's the latest form of camera).

If you view the new cameras as "electronic," Canon, Sony, and Hewlett-Packard have a better chance at being big in digital picture systems.

Because each emerging market segment has its own leader, Kodak, the leader in film photographic technology, has little chance of becoming the leader in the segment of digital photographic technology.

Kodak's best chance would be to buy or launch a new brand in this arena.

The Kodak brand would be reserved for film. The new brand or company would have no Kodak connection and would run on its own. Kodak's headquarters would be in Rochester. The new company would be headquartered somewhere in Silicon Valley.

This type of move might be hard for Kodak to swallow. But, if they try to turn their 100-year-old film brand into a digital brand, the future picture doesn't look very sharp.

Sears: Surrounded by Alligators

Sears is another century-old American icon that is suffering with a changing world. Not many years ago, there was a humorous observation that by the 1990s the Japanese would make everything and Sears would sell it. That turned out to be just a joke. Today, Sears has given up its leadership to Wal-Mart and a host of other competitors have surrounded them, each taking a bite out of Sears' different categories. To name but a few, there's Home Depot, Target, and Circuit City, as well as specialty retailers such as GAP, Old Navy, and even the full-service department stores that are aggressively trying to survive in an over-stored, over-malled retail environment.

That's exactly the challenge for Alan Lacey, the new 47-year-old CEO. In an opening interview in the *Wall Street Journal*, he criticized the long-gone "Softer Side of Sears" as focusing on just one part of the retailer's offerings. Nor does he like the current "Good life at a great price" strategy, which he feels is too price oriented. His question is, "Why should I go to Sears instead of Target"?

That is the right question, but I'm not so sure that the answer is focusing on the Sears name instead of the retail brands (one of his observations in that interview). First and foremost, he should understand what made Sears famous and successful and make that his starting point for the correct strategy.

What Made Sears Famous

No it wasn't the catalog. That was the correct answer several generations ago. In modern times, Sears was one of the few retailers, if not the only retailer, that built real brands. People went to Sears to buy Kenmore appliances, Craftsman tools, DieHard batteries, Weatherbeater paint, and Roadhandler tires.

Once there, they bought other stuff like Levi's or Sony TVs. But it was those brands, sold only at Sears, that made the difference.

But in recent years, there hasn't been much in the way of brand building coming out of Sears. Quite the contrary—"Brand Central" talked about offering everybody's brands (wrong strategy). And the "Soft Side" featured no brands (wrong strategy).

It would appear that Sears has not learned one of the lessons presented earlier: *Never forget what made you famous.*

Needed: Brand Refurbishing

Since there has been a hiatus in brand building at Sears, it seems obvious that what's needed is to revisit each brand and figure out how to revitalize and strengthen it. They should take advantage of Kenmore's leadership and position it as the number one family of appliances in the land. They should do the same for Craftsman, which is America's favorite brand of tools by far. Perhaps it's time for a next generation of DieHard battery that dies a little harder? Maybe their paints could use some sprucing up?

If they do a good job with their brands, more people will go to Sears. And if designers improve the store's layout, people might spend more time buying other things.

And while they're at it, maybe they should invest in a new brand or two? Something like cosmetics or a clothing line or even that specialty truck tire idea mentioned in Chapter 9. What I wouldn't do was spend a lot of money on the "Sears" brand. That's only where you go to find those "sold only at Sears" brands.

A Good Sign

Ironically, while the new Sears CEO started off the *Wall Street Journal* article with not such a hot idea, he ended it with exactly the right idea. Here's what was reported: *Mr. Lacey views Kenmore appliances, where Sears has strong sales and market shares, as a model to run around the rest of the retail business. In a meeting with retail analysts he said, "We have a case study we would like to implement elsewhere in our company."*

Now you're talking.

They're Not Alone

The big brands I've just put under the microscope are only a few among many that could be headed for big trouble.

How far can Apple Computer go on good looks and being different? Can a one-trick pony like Polaroid come up with another trick? Can Revlon ever climb out from beneath its massive debt load of more than a billion dollars? Will DaimlerChrysler ever figure out why they merged? For that matter, will AOL and Time Warner come up with a reason for their joining together? Will Amazon ever make any money?

But it's also important to look at some of the folks in the marketplace who often encourage trouble, for example, consultants who cost a lot but offer little help. And what about Wall Street's tendency to push companies into doing the wrong things?

With friends like these, you don't need competitors.

CHAPTER

13

An Army of Consultants

But No One to Help

While no one has the real number, it has been estimated that management consulting has a global market of more than $50 billion. Consultants are drawn to money like bees to honey. So big rich companies are surrounded by all types of consulting firms, trying to collect as much as they can to feed their expensive teams. (It costs about $250,000 a month to have one of McKinsey's consulting teams on site.)

Many of the big brands in trouble were surrounded by consultants who took their money but apparently offered no real help with the problems threatening to overwhelm them. From their performance with these big brands, one could accurately portray these folks as modern-day Robin Hoods: They rob from the rich and keep it.

Two Examples

Two examples from earlier chapters make the point. Levi's spent $850 million on Andersen Consultants to reengineer the company to serve the customer better. All this did was create chaos that made things worse. The board of directors finally had to stop the nonsense.

AT&T was reported to have spent over half a billion dollars on consultants between 1989 and 1994. To get a sense of how much money AT&T spent, consider the following numbers that were collected and reported in a wonderful book by James O'Shea and Charles Madigan (Penguin, 1998) on the subject of consultants entitled *Dangerous Company: Management Consultants and the Businesses They Save and Ruin* (a must read):

- McKinsey & Co. collected $96,349,000 during that period of time.
- Monitor, Michael Porter's Harvard-connected consulting business, gathered a total of $127 million from 1991 to 1994, collecting $58,817,000 of that amount in 1993 alone.
- Andersen Consulting collected $39,808,000 from AT&T in 1992 and $36,096,000 in 1993 ($87 million over four years).
- Hundreds of smaller companies collected millions upon millions as AT&T jumped from philosophy to philosophy such as "business transformation," "change management," or "business process reengineering."

So, what did AT&T get for all that money? It's now apparent that they learned very little to keep them out of trouble.

It's All a Mystery

Big consulting companies tend to create cultures that make them seem more like law firms than consulting businesses, with secrecy and "client privilege" being dominant themes. This has a legitimate purpose in that clients don't want their secrets discussed. But it also provides a perfect excuse for not talking about anything that might be uncomfortable.

One of my favorite consulting pitches comes from Monitor, a guru-driven consulting company with Michael Porter of Harvard fame at the top. They readily admit that most consulting engagements fail because of excessive promises. This invokes the law of candor: "Admit a negative and the prospect will give you a positive." The positive here is that they will "engender action" while creating long-term relationships. (Translation: We love to get our hooks into you.)

Needless to say, $127 million of engendered action didn't help AT&T very much.

The Hustling of Ideas

To make real money, a consultant has to have an idea to sell.

As the authors of *Dangerous Company* outline, the recipe for consulting success has four ingredients:

1. Get an article in the *Harvard Business Review.*
2. Pump it up into a book.
3. Pray for a best-seller.
4. Hustle the idea for all it's worth.

Firms like McKinsey can avoid being attached to any particular trend, but the consultants-come-late need a unique concept to hustle. But these aren't just ideas—they are called management tools. If you have any doubts about the size of this industry, just check out the following list of what could be called the "explosion of management tools":

ABC	Pay for Performance	SWOT
MBO	Customer	KSFs
TQM	Satisfaction Meas.	Benchmarking
JIT	Visioning	Life Cycle Analysis
OVA	Core Competencies	Excellence
SVA	Baldrige Award	Scenario Planning
CPR	Micro-Marketing	SPIRE
SPC	MRPI and MRPII	Kaizen
Kanban	Technology S-Curves	Learning
Reengineering	Delphi Technique	Organizations
Mass Customization	Gap Analysis	Environmental
System Dynamics	ISO 9000	Scanning
Workout	7-Ss	Metagame Analysis
Concurrent	6-Sigma	Horizontal
Engineering	5-Forces	Organizations
Zero-Based Budgets	4-Ps	Value Chain Analysis
PIMS Analysis	3-Cs	Nominal Group
Quality Circles	2 × 2 Matrices	Technique
DCF	1-Minute Managing	Conjoint Analysis
Portfolio Analysis	0-Defects	Competitive Gaming
Experience Curves	Empowerment	Customer Retention
Mission and Vision	Strategic Alliances	Groupware
Statements	Service Guarantees	Psychographics
Cycle Time	Self-Directed Teams	Loyalty Management
Reduction	Strategic Planning	

Some "Robin Hood Research"

Bain & Co. oversees a force of more than 1,300 consultants from their deluxe offices in Boston's Copley Place. They are so secretive they don't carry business cards. And it has been reported that when discussing clients on airplanes they use code words instead of names.

In recent years they have been researching the use of these many tools. And in a *Wall Street Journal* (May 21, 2001) article they advised business executives not to "get hammered by management fads." Most likely, it was a clever way to help companies sort out the good guys (theirs) from the bad guys (all the others). Bain felt that there was no objective data on whether increased tool usage was good or bad and which tools were producing results. Their point was that in the absence of data, groundless hype "makes choosing tools a dangerous game of choice" (absolutely).

When you consider that few people would acknowledge wasting hundreds of thousands of dollars on these efforts, I was startled to see that 81 percent of the 5,600 executives surveyed said that tools promised more than they delivered. (That's a politically correct way of saying, "We blew a lot of money.")

One problem with all these tools is that they are process driven. To use an automobile analogy, they are intended to get the corporate engine running more smoothly not to show how the car should be designed and promoted, which is what will spell success or failure. Another problem is that all of the company's competitors have access to the same tools. Michael Porter has written that these process-oriented tools aren't enough in today's competitive market. He does indeed talk about the need for a unique position but he never offers much help on what it takes to be unique.

At about the same time his organization was sucking millions out of AT&T, Ma Bell was plopping $10 billion into the obviously terrible strategy of buying NCR and of taking on IBM in the computer business. Where were Porter and his gang when help was desperately needed? He should have been in the CEO's office pointing out what was very bad strategy.

A good consultant has to search for what is right in the context of what a company can or cannot do. It has nothing to do with buzzwords or fancy processes But there's also an important lesson in all this.

 **Good leaders know where they are going.**

The three most popular tools in the Bain study were strategic planning, mission and vision statements, and benchmarking.

I've already explained why benchmarking is a trap. The trick is to be different, not the same as your competitors.

Strategy, vision, and mission statements are dependent on the simple premise that you must know where you're going. No one can follow you if you don't know where you're headed. Big companies are so encumbered with rules, traditions, and egos that top management is prone not to lead anyone anywhere. There aren't too many Jack Welch types pointing out the direction and setting the pace.

Peter Drucker had it right when he wrote in *The Effective Executive* (HarperBusiness, 1993): "The foundation of effective leadership is thinking through the organization's mission, defining it and establishing it, clearly and visibly. The leader sets the goals, sets the priorities, and sets and maintains the standards."

He didn't write, "First you hire some consultants to help you work out your vision and mission statements."

Also, the best leaders know that direction alone is no longer enough. They don't have an army of McKinsey types roaming the halls and undermining morale. They themselves are in the halls acting as cheerleaders, storytellers, and facilitators. They reinforce their sense of direction or vision with words or action.

I've told this story before, but it's worth retelling in the context of this lesson.

There is no greater leader in the airline business than Herb Kelleher, the chairman of Southwest Airlines. He has become the king of the low-fare, short-haul airline business. Year after year, his airline is on every list of the "most admired" and "most profitable" companies.

Anybody who knows Herb realizes that the airline's personality is Herb's personality. He is an amazing cheerleader who keeps those planes moving and morale high. He is indeed "walking behind them." He also knows his people and his business. In a meeting with Herb, we were encouraging him to buy one of the East Coast shuttles up for sale. It would instantly make Southwest a big player in the East.

He thought a minute and said, "I sure would like their gates in New York, Washington, and Boston. But what I don't want is their airplanes, and more importantly their people."

He sure was right. Cheerleading those East Coast shuttle people would have been impossible. And he didn't need a consultant's report to tell him that.

Indirect Damage

Consultants can have a negative impact on a company even when they do a good job. One of the interesting stories in *Dangerous Company* was about Sears. They touted Arthur Martinez as an enlightened CEO who didn't believe in the typical broad-brush strategy engagements. As the authors reported, Martinez was against the "Come help me figure out what I should do with this company" approach.

After the first round of internal cost-cutting was finished, Mr. Martinez looked at the money being spent with suppliers of the products being made for Sears. Obviously, it was a lot. How could they reduce their vendors' costs à la Wal-Mart? So he hired the consulting company of A.T. Kearney to go in and push "best manufacturing practices" among their suppliers. These are code words that mean finding ways to encourage vendors to reduce their costs. Kearney would go through a supplier's plant from top to bottom and come up with an assessment of how it could be improved to cut costs.

Nice idea with, sometimes, bad consequences.

The DieHard Saga

Kearney showed up at Johnson Controls Inc., a company that had been making DieHard Batteries for 25 years and made an assessment that Sears could save 20 percent in costs of batteries with improved manufacturing practices.

How could a CEO say "No" to that?

When asked to reduce their costs, Johnson Controls declined and lost the business to other suppliers. But then, a not-so-funny thing happened. The market began to notice that DieHard's quality was dropping and they weren't dying quite as hard. (Hey, when you squeeze costs 20 percent, something has to give.)

Losing a little quality might not be a big deal in most situations, but this is a big problem for Sears. DieHard is one of their premium brands with a premier reputation. This must be protected at all costs because it is brands like DieHard, Kenmore, Craftsman, and Weatherbeater paint that make the difference for Sears versus Wal-Mart or Home Depot. It's the only place to get these highly respected products. To squeeze out quality is to weaken these brands. To weaken them is to weaken Sears.

Although Kearney did its cost-cutting job, indirectly it also did some damage. But let's get back to another important lesson.

 ### Consultants are rarely candid about mistakes.

Even if consultants spot a bad strategy and have doubts about it, rarely will they run the risk of alienating their client who cooked it up. When their objective is to get into what they call a long-term relationship, they certainly don't want to risk it by being brutally honest about a client mistake. Millions are at stake, so consultants tend to leave their best tool out in the parking lot. It's called "objectivity."

If you look that word up in the dictionary, it means "without bias or prejudice; detached; impersonal." As outsiders, the role of consultants is to cut through all the bias, personal agendas, and personalities that surround many tough decisions. They can't be in a "protect their billings" mode because they then have a conflict of interest on their hands. They have introduced their own organization's bias into the equation and hindered their ability to truly help a client by being honest and objective. (This same principle also causes advertising agencies to be less than candid.)

Good consultants put down on paper what they think is right as they see it. They shouldn't worry about reaction or whether a client will like this or dislike that. And they should avoid concerning themselves about the compromises that might be needed to make the recommendation acceptable. There probably isn't an executive in the company who doesn't know how to make compromises with little outside help. What they really need is some help on what "right" is. Then they will be able to make the appropriate compromise.

Now, let's say you've come across a rare consultant who is indeed objective and even brutally honest. Are you out of the woods? Will the right advice be forthcoming? The next lesson says there's a good chance it won't be.

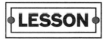 ## Consultants rarely understand the mind of the customer.

The problem is one of training. Marketing battles take place in the mind of a customer or prospect. That's where you win. That's where you lose. It's all about positioning your brand or company in the mind. It's also about understanding the following six principles on how the mind works and the psychology behind people's decisions (see *The New Positioning* [McGraw-Hill, 1995] for more):

1. Minds can't cope.
2. Minds are limited.
3. Minds hate confusion.
4. Minds are insecure.
5. Minds don't change.
6. Minds can lose focus.

Your bright MBA consultant has had little or no training on this subject. What he gets trained on is understanding and getting into the minds of the CEO and the board. It's like going to war but not knowing how to shoot.

Michael Porter uses the word "positioning," but he doesn't know much about the process of differentiating a brand in the mind. Nor is he interested in learning. (I once was the speaker just ahead of him at a big management conference. He didn't even come in to listen.) He sees what I do as "marketing" and what he does as "strategy." Will someone please explain the difference? To me, marketing brings strategy to life in the mind of the prospect.

If Porter or his people understood the mind, they would have said to AT&T that people see them as a telephone, not a computer. And since minds don't change, there is no chance of success whatever they do in the computer business. That advice could have saved their client a great deal of money (billions) and effort.

The troubles described in earlier chapters were mostly caused by companies and their consultants not recognizing that perceptual problems were at the heart of their difficulties:

- General Motors did not recognize they were causing customer confusion by pricing their cars alike and making them look alike.
- Xerox tried to convince the minds in the marketplace that they could make computers. Any Xerox machine that couldn't make a copy did not compute in the mind.
- Digital Equipment failed to build perceptions in the marketplace that 64-bit workstations were the "next thing."
- Levi Strauss did not exploit its pioneering position by making the competitors nothing but copies in the minds of their customers.
- Crest did not evolve in the mind from "cavity prevention" to the perception of being "the pioneer in toothcare."

- Burger King did not hang the perception of "kiddieland" on McDonald's and make "flame broiled" the essence of a grown-up burger.

- Firestone, long-term, was not able to overcome a massive amount of negative publicity that built perceptions of their tires being unsafe.

- Miller failed to understand that it can be only one thing in the mind, not nine things.

If that army of consultants had understood that strategy is a battle for the minds of their customers and prospects, they would easily have spotted the preceding problems, and those big companies could have avoided big trouble.

It reminds me of a wonderful little story about a consultant.

The Shepherd and the Consultant

A shepherd is herding his flock in a remote pasture when suddenly a brand-new Jeep Cherokee advances out of a dust cloud toward him. The driver, a young man in a Brioni suit, Gucci shoes, Ray-Ban sunglasses and a YSL tie leans out of the window and asks:

"If I can tell you exactly how many sheep you have in your flock, will you give me one?"

The shepherd looks at the yuppie, then at his peacefully grazing flock and calmly answers "sure."

The yuppie parks the car, whips out his notebook, connects it to a cell-phone, surfs to a NASA page on the Internet where he calls up a GPS satellite navigation system, scans the area, opens up a database and some 60 Excel spreadsheets with complex formulas. Finally he prints out a 150-page report on his hi-tech miniaturized printer, turns around to the shepherd, and says: "You have here exactly 1,586 sheep."

"This is correct. As agreed you can take one of the sheep," says the shepherd. He watches the young man make a selection and bundle it into his Cherokee. Then he says: "If I can tell you exactly what your business is, will you give me my sheep back?"

"Okay, why not" answers the young man.

"You are a consultant," says the shepherd.

"That is correct," says the yuppie. "How did you guess that?"

"Easy" answers the shepherd. "You turn up here although nobody called you. You want to be paid for the answer to a question I already knew the solution to. And you don't know anything about my business because you took my dog."

CHAPTER 14

Boards of Directors

But No One to Help

O ne would think that the last line of defense against bad decisions would be the board of directors. Here you have a dozen or so wise people with decades of experience ready to keep the CEO and his senior executives on the straight and narrow. Right? Wrong.

It would appear that this certainly is not the case. In recent years, boards certainly seem ready to fire the CEO if the numbers go bad. Jill Barad's hasty departure from Mattel came just three years after she got to the top. Douglas Ivestor left Coca-Cola after only two years at the helm. Robert Anunziata exited Global Crossing after only 53 weeks. Richard Thoman was unceremoniously fired from Xerox after just three years on the job (more on this in Chapter 15).

But, where was the board when all the wrong decisions were being made? The only way to avoid big trouble is to nip bad decisions in the bud, not when they are fully flowered and showing signs of rapidly wilting.

Asleep at the Wheel

As described in Chapter 3, the troubles at Xerox go way back. Decades of bad decisions have brought this once high-flying company to the brink. As one effort after another to penetrate the computer market failed or as Hewlett-Packard's laser printing business soared on an invention of Xerox, one would think that the board would have stepped in sooner.

But perhaps they were all too busy serving on other boards to stop and raise the right questions. Seven directors out of Xerox's 15 members sit on five or more boards. Paul Allaire, the long-time Xerox CEO, sits on five boards. Xerox president and Chief Operating Officer Anne Mulcahy sits on four boards. Vernon Jordan, of Bill Clinton fame, sits on eleven boards. That is far too much, especially for the Xerox situation, because the problems there demand the full attention of the officers.

In addition, 5 of the 15 members are insiders who are busy defending their decisions. And the rest certainly didn't have much in the way of strategic experience. They included an ex-admiral, several lawyers, a banker from Germany, a woman from Lucent Technologies, and several financial people. There were executives from Johnson & Johnson and Procter & Gamble on the board, but they were lacking in technical marketing expertise. So it's no surprise that this group hung back until it was too late to keep Xerox out of big trouble.

The Wrong Experience

When you study the composition of boards, you wonder how these people get selected. Vernon Jordan is a Washington insider so folks might figure he could help open doors. The same goes for ex-President Gerald Ford and Henry Kissinger. But none of these members can be of much help in preventing companies from making faulty decisions.

Just for fun, I looked to see who was on AT&T's board. Here's a company that has desperately needed some help. Besides the insiders, I found a retired oil company executive, an economic consultant, a retired textile company CEO, the chairman of Kodak (a company in some trouble), a retired Caterpillar Company executive, an international relations consultant, a law professor, the CEO of Citigroup (he is kept pretty busy with his own organization), and a former CEO of CBS who didn't do very well there.

No one in that group had the technical or marketing background to challenge the earlier decision to take on IBM in computers or Mr. Armstrong's $100 billion vision of buying cable companies as the reentry into the homes they had to give up to the Baby Bells years ago.

Very few boards have the talent or experience to be of much help before the fact. They can pick up the pieces but have little ability to keep things from being broken.

Friends and Cronies

And what makes things worse is appointing folks whose only claim to fame is knowing the CEO. At Walt Disney Corporation you'll find a lot of friends and acquaintances on the board. CEO Michael Eisner has appointed his attorney, his architect, the principal of the elementary school once attended by his children, and the president of a university that received a $1 million donation.

Business Week (March 5, 2001) rates the worst and best boards every year. Here's what they had to say about some of their perennial losers:

> Disney isn't the only hardy perennial to show up on the wrong side
> of the governance fence. Other repeat performers include Archer

Daniels Midland Co. and Advanced Micro Devices Inc. ADM has only five independent directors out of a dozen and, like Advanced Micro, also has at least one nonindependent board member on its nominating, compensation, and audit committees. Governance experts say the work of these key committees should be done solely by outsiders to quash potential conflicts of interest. And two new-comers, Rite Aid Corp. and Cendant Corp., show up just behind Disney in the No. 2 and No. 4 spots. Accounting scandals at both concerns led to management upheavals and probes by the Securi-ties & Exchange Commission. These problems have raised serious questions about their boards. At Rite Aid, which has restated its fi-nancial results for the previous three years, the audit committee met only twice in fiscal 1999. Four of the company's nine directors were insiders, and five board members are 70 or older. "It's a cor-porate government nightmare," says Stanford's Koppes.

Obviously, no one here is watching out for the stockholders very much. It's enough to make you want to put all your money into CDs and government bonds.

Excessive Generosity with Shareholders' Money

Just how "friendly" a board can be to the CEO can be measured in the money they give to the boss. Archer Daniels Midland, a global power in agricultural commodities, set the record for friendliness. ADM pleaded guilty to federal price-fixing charges in 1996 and paid a $100 million fine, the largest ever in a price-fixing case. So when the feds, who had it all on videotape, brought criminal price-fixing charges against two former ADM executives and a current one, Michael Andreas (son of longtime CEO Dwayne Andreas), you would figure that there was substance behind the charges. All three pleaded not guilty and went to trial, and the company placed Michael Andreas on a paid leave of absence. (So if you get indicted at ADM, you still get paid; you just don't work.) When Andreas and the other two were convicted, he went on an unpaid leave. So if you're a felon, you're still an employee.

Now that's what I call friendly. A similar case happened when I was at General Electric many years ago. The convicted executives went off to jail and were no longer employees.

Occidental Petroleum is a legend and is considered by experts to be the all-time champ at shareholder abuse. How's this for an example of generosity? In 1997, the board bought out the remaining seven years of CEO Ray Iran's contract for $95 million; then, having in effect paid him for the next seven years at the rate of $13 million a year, they give him a new contract that guarantees him $1.2 million a year. (And this guy doesn't even play baseball.)

This all led to a shareholder suit, which forced Oxy into a massive overhaul of its governance. Has this improved performance? So far, the company has performed worse than its peer group, which suggests that even under duress, their board isn't of much help with the business.

A Nightmare Underway

Warnaco is a company in big trouble. It's another example of awesome pay for awful performance.

Warnaco is an apparel maker whose brands include Calvin Klein, Speedo, Chaps, Olga, and many others. Last year they lost $338 million and the stock has seen most of its value evaporate. Yet, despite this, CEO Linda Wachner received a stunning pay package in 1998.

Her base salary of $2.7 million was the second highest I could find anywhere, behind only Jack Welch's $2.8 million at GE. Her bonus of $6 million, was bigger than Jacques Nasser's at Ford, where the stock rose 70 percent that year, or Lee Raymond's at Exxon, where the stock went up and where Raymond negotiated what was then the largest merger ever. Wachner also received $6.5 million in restricted stock, plus millions of reload options—which are automatically replaced every time one is exercised. Bottom line: She was paid as if she had a knockout year running a huge company, when in fact Warnaco, too small for the Fortune 500, lost money, and its stock lost value. At last word, the auditors were questioning the company's viability.

The board's composition is the kind that makes corporate-governance experts cringe. Of the seven members, two are insiders; of the five outsiders, two are consultants to the company and one is an attorney to the company. Warnaco stock remains in the tank, suggesting a powerful need to shake up the firm if even that is possible.

You have to wonder how things ever got so bad at these companies. The answer is that throwing out a bad board requires considerable effort and coordination by shareholders—usually mutual funds and pension funds—that, for business or political reasons, may not want to get tough with the directors of large companies. Still, shareholders will take only so much and eventually they sue.

It's a lot better to start with a good board than to try and get rid of a bad board. So, what would make up a good board?

A Board of Specialists

If I were looking for a board, the last thing I'd want would be old buddies, celebrities, or retired CEOs. I would choose a group of people who could be of real help in keeping my company out of trouble. That means I would want experts in the various functions important to my business. Here's the kind of lineup I would seek:

- A *financial expert.* Wall Street, capital requirements, financial reporting, and currency variations are just a few of the needs that have to be accommodated. It sure would be nice to have an outsider with some experience in this field looking over my numbers and making suggestions on how to improve them.
- A *manufacturing expert.* If I happen to be making something, having someone that knows his or her way around factories and has a sense of the latest technology would certainly be a big help. This would be especially helpful if new technology was involved.

- A *human resources expert.* Large companies are nothing but collections of people. The care, feeding, and educating of my team is critical. This kind of backup would be helpful to my own people in tune with the latest organizational ideas in the field.

- A *marketing expert.* All the world is a marketing problem and I would like to have a board member who could seriously question what we're up to in terms of planning. I'd like to know if he or she sees some serious problems. What I don't want are people to rubber-stamp our plans.

- A *management expert.* An ex-CEO in a related field could be of help or even someone out of the consulting or academic world who has been around and seen the good, the bad, and the ugly in the corporate world. Once again, I'd look for someone who is brutally honest and willing to tell my people or me that we have to improve our organization.

While this may be a dream team, what I am after is a group of objective outsiders who bring some real skills to the board. What I'm not after are famous names, people who just make the board politically correct (women, minorities, etc.), or people who simply agree with me.

It's an increasingly difficult world out there, and you need all the help you can get.

Boards Should Be Involved

I am being a little unfair to all those boards out there. Many cannot be of any help because top management rarely involves them in making those good or bad decisions. They usually see things only when they are ready for the rubber stamp.

My one experience where a board was involved in the thinking process worked out very well. I had been asked into some strategic work being done at Continental Airlines by Don Valentine, an

excellent marketing executive with whom I had worked at Southwest Airlines. His assignment was to help develop a short-haul, low-
price competitor to Southwest similar to what United eventually
did with their United Shuttle service on the West Coast. A proto-
type was developed using the "Continental Peanut Fares" name and
the issue was whether to use CALITE (Continental Airlines Lite)
as a subbrand or create a totally new name.

"Continental" Was the Problem

Our presentation was not very enthusiastic about a Southwest type
of subbrand. First of all, they didn't have a lot of what Southwest
had such as Herb Kelleher, one kind of plane, no hubs, and no
reservation system or the lowest cost per mile in the industry. Second, a lot of low-fare airlines were about to be born (this all happened in the mid-1990s). Since Continental had been in and out
of bankruptcy, there was a need to reposition the Continental
brand and not try to launch a new Southwest type brand.

My recommendation was to position Continental against the big
three (American, United, and Delta) as having "More airline for
the money." Forget about "CALITE" or "Peanut Fares"; focus on
the main brand.

Next Up: The Board

While this wasn't something that the CEO wanted to hear, Don
Valentine encouraged him to show this presentation to the board.
He agreed.

The meeting didn't go especially well as the CEO certainly
wasn't wildly enthusiastic about trying to position Continental as
having more value and abandoning the "Peanut Fares" effort. At
the end of the meeting, I was packing up and one of the board
members came up to me and thanked me for the presentation. I expressed my feelings that it hadn't gone very well. She said, "Not at
all. We heard you."

And indeed they had. CALITE never happened, new management was brought in, and they did indeed offer more airline for the money with a more rewarding frequent flyer program, less expensive first-class service, and newer airplanes.

They are doing very well these days, and I would have to give a lot of credit to the board on this one. They were of real help.

CHAPTER 15

Wall Street

Nothing but Trouble

If consultants and boards of directors are of little help, at least they don't cause too much damage. Occasionally, they even produce some good thinking. But those friendly folks from Wall Street often create an environment that encourages bad, sometimes irrevocable, things to happen. In a way, they set up a greenhouse for trouble, and like a greenhouse, what it's all about is encouraging things to "grow."

Growth Can Be a Problem

The well-known economist Milton Friedman put it perfectly when he said, "We don't have a desperate need to grow. We have a desperate desire to grow." That desire for growth is at the heart of what

169

can go wrong for many companies. Growth is the by-product of doing things right. But in itself, it is not a worthy goal. In fact, growth is the culprit behind impossible goals.

CEOs pursue growth to ensure their tenures and to increase their take-home pay. Wall Street brokers pursue growth to ensure their reputations and to increase their take-home pay.

But is it all necessary? Not really. When you consider that people do damaging things to force unnecessary growth, you can say that it's a crime against the brand. A true story illustrates how the desire for growth is at the root of evil doings.

I was brought in to evaluate business plans for a large multi-brand drug company. In turn, the brand managers stood up and presented their next year's plans. In the course of a presentation, a young executive warned of aggressive new competition in his category that would definitely change the balance of power. But when it came to a sales projection, there was a predicted 15 percent increase. Instantly, I questioned how this could be with the new competition.

His answer was they were going to do some short-term maneuvering and line extension. Long-term, wouldn't this hurt the brand? Well, yes. Then why do it? Because his boss made him put in the increase, and I would have to talk with him.

One week later, the boss admitted the problem but said his boss needed the increase because of, you guessed it, Wall Street.

The 15 Percent Delusion

Carol Loomis, a well-known *Fortune* editor, wrote a landmark article on this subject that challenged the "brash predictions about earnings growth that often lead to missed targets, battered stock and creative accounting." The question asked: Why can't CEOs kick the habit?

In the article, Carol laid out what has become accepted executive behavior:

Of all the goals articulated, the most common one among good-sized companies is annual growth in earnings per share of 15 percent—the equivalent, you might say, of making the all star team. With 15 percent growth, a company will roughly double its earnings in five years. It will almost inevitably star in the stock market, and its CEO will be given, so to speak, ticker-tape parades. (February 5, 2001)

You don't have to be a rocket scientist to figure out why this happens. It's these kinds of predictions that get Wall Street's attention. It's like a love dance between Wall Street and management as they whisper sweet nothings to each other. Management wants the top analysts to follow them and recommend their stock. Wall Street wants a winner to make analysts look good and attract more money. But, there is no reality in all this.

It's all a delusion.

The Real Numbers

As Loomis points out in her article, extensive research shows that few companies are able to grow 15 percent or higher a year. Over the past 40 years, *Fortune* looked at 150 companies for three basic time periods (1960–1980, 1970–1990, 1989–1999).

In each of those time frames, only three or four companies achieved the 15 percent or more earnings growth factor. About 20 to 30 companies ran at a 10 percent to 15 percent clip, 40 to 60 companies ran at 5 percent to 10 percent, 20 to 30 at 0 to 5 percent, and 20 to 30 actually ran a negative number. That's right, there were as many big losers as big winners.

Overall, during that 40-year period, the aftertax profits grew at an annual rate of just over 8 percent. This means that any company doing 15 percent was running at almost twice the rate as the general population of companies.

With that reality, it's not surprising that companies start to do some bad things to keep their growth rate up.

The Tricks of the Trade

The easiest way to keep Wall Street at bay is to ignore special charges that the accountants can handle with some small print beneath that ever-rising earnings chart. Another is to rob from next quarter to look good this quarter. This often involves "trade loading" or stuffing distribution channels with goods at the end of the quarter to push up sales. Or the gambit of declaring an overfunded pension and cutting contributions.

But what does the most long-term damage is the pressure, as described earlier, to grow the brand by pushing line extensions. While this approach doesn't help short-term earnings, management often sees it as a way to get bigger by getting a piece of another market.

This kind of activity gradually undermines the essence of what makes a brand different and successful. Nothing dramatizes this as much as the venerable Porsche brand.

A Porsche SUV?

That's almost a contradiction in terms, but Porsche wants to cash in on the sport-utility phenomenon and use it to, you guessed it, grow. (And it's not about making money. On average in 2000, General Motors earned $853 for every car it sold. Porsche earned about $7,350.) That means they will introduce the Cayenne, which will be the size of a Jeep Grand Cherokee. It's the first non-sports car in its 53-year history and it will have four doors, four seats, and a tailgate. (It's hard to believe.) In the mind, a Porsche is the classic 911, the rear engine, air-cooled, 6-cylinder car. Porsche doesn't want to face this reality and keeps trying to extend its line.

In the 1970s and 1980s, it tried to move downscale, first by building a mid-engine car with Volkswagen, the 914; and then a front-engine car with Audi, the 924. Both were eventually discontinued. In 1978, Porsche introduced a front-engine, V-8 powered 928 that was supposed to replace the archaic rear-engined 911. But purists refused to accept the 928 as a true Porsche, so it was discontinued. To this day, the 911 motors on.

One would think that Porsche would get the message that any car that doesn't look like the 911 isn't a Porsche to those in the market for one. Nope. They're back working with Volkswagen on a car that is about as far away from the 911 as you can get.

Good luck.

McDonald's "New Tastes" Menu?

At McDonald's, the golden arches aren't looking so golden these days. In 2000, sales grew just 3 percent and fourth-quarter net earnings declined 7 percent. This hasn't helped its stock, which is near a two-year low.

So CEO Jack Greenberg has done what most red-blooded CEOs would do: He is rolling out something called a New Tastes Menu—a collection of 44 items to be rotated four-at-a-time by franchisees. He hopes this will help double U.S. sales over the next 10 years. The problem is that much of this stuff isn't "new." It contains some old seasonal products like the McRib and the Shamrock Shake (it's green). Also included are what appear to be some Wendy's knockoffs like a strip of bacon or some ranch dressing. The Quarter Pounder with cheese comes with three kinds of cheese—cheddar, Swiss, and American.

All this will do is produce lines at every cash register and a number of complaints about those slow-moving lines.

Good luck.

Insidious Stock Options

Where Wall Street often sneaks into the equation is in the form of stock options. When management or even middle-level employees are looking at their stock options, they start to get concerned about that next quarter. They want to make sure their options stay healthy, so they are quick to cut corners or not make a long-term decision that is good for the business but could take several cents off earnings. They read the papers. You miss your earnings estimate by a few pennies and Wall Street will take your stock down 20 percent. That could put those options underwater and create an army of employees with very long faces.

A client of mine in the pizza business reported just such an example of short-term versus long-term thinking. One of his people had come across a new flour milling system that dramatically improved the dough-making process. The people in charge hung back from quickly spending the money on what the owner thought was the right thing to do. The reason for the delay was that the costs would impact quarterly earnings estimates. As he put it, "My people were robbing from Peter (quality improvement) to pay Paul (Wall Street)."

Needless to say, he's trying to get away from the options method of paying his people.

Ego Problems

Another thing that happens to CEOs when they miss their brave but unrealistic goals is that their ego takes a hit at the same time their stock takes a hit. With all the financial news reporting out there, Wall Street's devaluing of a stock puts the CEO in the glaring light of bad publicity. Suddenly, everyone is writing stories about this CEO and how he missed his numbers.

One day Carly Fiorina is a hero at Hewlett-Packard; the next day they are writing about her overambitious targets and how she is losing her credibility with Wall Street. If you're thick of skin, it's no big deal. But guess who reads those same articles? The board of directors and your employees. Taking a public hit like that erodes your reputation and wears on you. It makes you cautious, which isn't always such a good thing. Think how a general would feel if he started getting negative press right in the middle of a campaign? It certainly wouldn't encourage much more boldness on his part. That in turn could turn out to be a big plus for the enemy.

Encourage Them, Then Dump Them

In recent years, the fickleness of Wall Street has also caused havoc in many industries.

The process starts step is when the investment bankers move in and start to encourage companies to spend money on what they see as a quick way to go public and make some big gains. We all saw this in the dot-com craze, which was analogous to the gold rush. But as soon as the world realized that there was no gold in those hills (with the exception of the pornography mountain), Wall Street quickly turned off the money spigot and the crash ensued. What was sad is that it didn't take any particular skill to spot that almost all the dot-com business plans had little hope of ever turning a profit. What was driving all this was the hope of making a profit on the stock.

Tel-com Hell

Next up was Wall Street and the DSL craze (Digital Subscriber Line). These lines were going to thrust antiquated phone lines into the digital broadband era. Consumers would be able to download Web pages at speeds 26 times as fast as "dial-up" services. Phone companies could compete with cable modems.

Instead of this new golden age of telecommunications, bankruptcy courts are flooded with filings from North Point, Zyan, and dozens of other firms providing DSL. As an article in *Forbes* pointed out, installing these lines turned out to be a "Highway to Hell." It quickly became apparent that these carriers were nowhere near positive cash flow on each subscriber, but as the article pointed out:

The stock market didn't care. Wall Street valued these firms at as much as 250 times sales. The only important number was line growth. "We were highly incented by Wall Street to spend money like drunken sailors," says Elizabeth Fetter, North Point's chief executive. So everyone did. (February 19, 2001)

The money has dried up. The party is now over, and Wall Street is in search of its next place to generate some huge fees.

The Blind Leading the Blind

The hard truth is that many of these analysts just don't know very much about how to build a brand and a business. They've never had to do it. They don't understand that it's not about numbers or technology. It's about unique ideas and perceptions and successfully navigating the treacherous waters of competition.

But they bravely make their case in a highly visible way that has made many of them stock market rock stars. Such was the case of 41-year-old Mary Meeker, Morgan Stanley's internet analyst. *Fortune* magazine actually did a rather embarrassing front-page story on Ms. Meeker that raised questions about whether analysts can be trusted.

The article pointed out that Meeker's record points to a reluctance to recommend selling technology stocks. While she still expresses confidence in the market and its ability to rebound, one suspects that if you have been out there pushing a stock, and a 30-something mutual fund manager is buying a million shares of that stock, you just might be reluctant to change your mind. It does all work out to the blind (Buy it, I don't know where it's going) leading the blind (I'll buy it, but I don't know where it's going).

One Analyst That Gets It

There is one person on Wall Street who appears to understand a lot more about what goes into success or failure in a brand. His name is

Steve Milunovich. He has won many industry plaudits and is a technology strategist at Merrill Lynch. (You met him in the DEC story.)

What is unusual about Steve is that through the years he has been an avid reader of my books and will often call for my view on such and such a company. What he is trying to analyze is not just the numbers but also the marketing strategy behind those numbers.

What's even more unusual, he is the *only* analyst who has ever called to inquire who I thought was in trouble or not in trouble.

If Steve makes a recommendation, I listen carefully to it. As for the rest of them, good luck.

Some Defensive Advice

If your company is publicly held, Wall Street is a factor with which you must deal. The trick is how to avoid trouble in those dealings. Here are some tips from CEOs who have been burned. Their names have been omitted to protect them from retaliation against their stock.

- *Estimate low. Come in high.* The worst thing you can do is set unrealistic goals, even if you see it as a stretch for your people to "shoot for." The problem is that if you miss it, Wall Street will come back and take shots at you for missing your target, unrealistic or not. It's better to underpromise and overdeliver. Sure, they won't be as excited up front, but you won't get your stock dumped.

- *Reduce the number of analyst meetings.* The less you have to say, the less trouble you'll get into. I've yet to find a business that really runs on a quarter-to-quarter basis. And most important marketing moves take months or even years to pay off. So why all the chatter? My favorite CEO says that twice a year is enough. When his people attend these meetings, they begin to think that they should pursue the analysts' questions and advice. His position is that he wants them to think about the business not the numbers. So why taint them with this kind of thinking?

- *Talk strategy, not numbers.* When you have to have those meetings, try to spend as much time as possible talking about the strategy you're pursuing against your competition. The point is that if your strategy works, the numbers will follow. This tends to put the discussion on your turf as opposed to their turf. Remember, very few analysts understand this kind of stuff so you will have better control of the meetings. Besides, that's how a good business is run. Good generals don't have meetings to discuss casualties and enemy killed. They talk about the moves that are planned against the enemy.

The Joy of Being Privately Held

Did you ever wonder why those very successful privately held companies such as Milliken or Gore-Tex rarely show up in the press? That's because no one is staring at their numbers quarter after quarter. All they have to worry about is their business. And if they are happy with it, that's all that matters. It reminds me of yet another story:

The Tico Fisherman and the Wall Street Analyst

An American businessman was at the pier of a small coastal Costa Rican village when a small boat with just one fisherman docked. Inside the small boat were several large yellow fin tuna.

The American complimented the Costa Rican Tico on the quality of his fish and asked how long it took to catch them.

The Tico replied, "only a little while." The American then asked why he didn't stay out longer and catch more fish. The Tico said he had enough to support his family's immediate needs.

The American then asked, "But what do you do with the rest of your time?"

The Tico fisherman said, "I sleep late, fish a little, play with my children, take siesta with my wife Maria, stroll into the village each evening where I sip wine and play guitar with my amigos. I have a full and busy life, señor."

The American scoffed, "I am a Wall Street executive and could help you. You should spend more time fishing and with the proceeds buy a bigger boat and a Web presence. A scaleable go-forward plan would provide capital for several new boats. Eventually you would have a fleet of fishing boats. Instead of selling your catch to a middleman, you would sell directly to the processor, eventually opening your own cannery. You would control the product, processing, and distribution. You would need to leave this small coastal fishing village and move to San Jose, Costa Rica, then Los Angeles, and eventually New York City, where you would outsource tasks to third-party clients to help run your expanding enterprise in a vertical market."

The Tico fisherman asked, "But señor, how long will this all take?"

To which the American replied, "15–20 years."

"But what then, señor?"

The American laughed and said, "That's the best part. When the time is right, you will announce an IPO and sell your company stock to the public and become very rich. You will make millions."

"Millions, señor? Then what?"

The American said, "Then you will retire, move to a small coastal fishing village where you can sleep late, fish a little, play with your kids, take siesta with your wife, and stroll to the village in the evenings where you will sip wine and play your guitar with your amigos."

CHAPTER 16

Knowing Your Enemy Can Keep You Out of Trouble

At this point, you might be saying to yourself, "Isn't there a simpler way to stay out of trouble?" That's a good question. You cannot expect to measure every big decision against all the lessons I've just written about. What if you forget one? After all, very few people can remember most of the Ten Commandments once they get beyond stealing, killing, and adultery. People probably continue to do bad things in life and in marketing because the rules are sometimes unmanageable.

So I will condense this approach to one simple rule that isn't perfect but will tend to keep you from making mistakes: *Know your competitors.*

Now that might sound too obvious. Of course, you have to want to know your competitor. And what big company doesn't? Well, this might come as a shock, but many of those troubled brands that I've just written about either didn't recognize or badly underestimated their most important enemy in the marketplace:

- General Motors never saw the German or the Japanese small cars as threats. Instead, they ended up competing with their own brands. By the time they got around to the Saturn, it was too late.
- Xerox thought IBM was their enemy when it was Hewlett-Packard and the laser printer that did them in.
- Digital Equipment never saw the desktop computer as having the potential to undermine their minicomputer franchise. Once IBM's PC was established, DEC's days were numbered.
- AT&T never saw MCI and Sprint as the legitimate competitors they became. They never exploited the technological differences.
- Levi's never saw cheaper, me-too jeans as something that could overwhelm them in a category they invented.
- Crest never saw Colgate climbing back into the lead with their anticavity, antiplaque, antigingivitis toothpaste.
- Burger King never saw McDonald's as the enemy that they had to continue to attack. Once they backed off, they were run over.
- Marks & Spencer never took its new competitors seriously. They didn't think any enemy was going to threaten them.

While each case has its extenuating circumstances, the one thing that could have kept these companies out of trouble would have been a clearer perspective on the enemy. Because with this, you know what to do before you get into trouble.

Let's look at a big company that I wouldn't yet put on the troubled list, but is indeed at a crossroads. We'll use this "Know thy enemy" approach to evaluate their current moves.

Whither Hewlett-Packard?

HP has been a management icon for six decades. Its slow-growing mode in recent years led the board to find a hard-charging CEO who could lead the company from the likes of a near-death experience similar to the one that IBM endured 10 years ago and that Xerox is going through now.

They chose Carly Fiorina, a nonstop worker who only occasionally takes a break to have some glamorous pictures taken for the business magazines that are falling all over her. And she certainly isn't shy when it comes to analyzing the situation. In a *Business Week* article (February 19, 2001), she stated "We looked in the mirror and saw a great company that was becoming a failure."

Carly Fiorina's Plan

This same article went on to describe the steps she has taken and plans to take in turning HP into a winner in today's fiercely competitive technology market. Here are the highlights of how she plans to turn a dinosaur into a dynamo:

- Consolidate advertising from 43 agencies into two and relaunch the brand. This resulted in the "Invent" campaign and that little garage.
- Fold HP's 83 product divisions into four units that work with two sales and marketing units.
- Trigger new product categories in new Internet-related businesses, such as digital imaging and wireless services.

She is also whacking costs down by using more of the Web. But rumblings are already in the wind about all this aggressive management makeover as being too much, too soon for a company of this size. All it will do is cause confusion.

Well, I won't get into all that, but I don't have a sense of any meaningful strategy in all this. As best I can tell, it's all about we're going to get better and invent some new stuff. That's fine. But who is the enemy here? Knowing that helps set the proper strategic direction.

The End of Schizophrenia

Nobody talks much about it, but the first move was a brilliant one.

For years, every time I went out to HP on some project or other, I was always struck with the fact that Hewlett-Packard could never decide what kind of company it was. Were they a big measurement and testing company or a big computer company? Of course, it was both. By finally spinning off the test and measurement business, they cleared up their split personality dilemma. (The only thing that wasn't so smart was the strange, unpronounceable name of "Agilent." But that's another problem.)

Now, Hewlett-Packard could position themselves where DEC once was before their demise. Today, they are *the world's second largest computer company.* This is an impressive place to be, but more than that it clearly tells them who the enemy is and what strategy to pursue.

"Relaunching the brand" is simply an exercise in making people aware that HP is number two in an enormous category. It shouldn't have been a program about inventing things in that little garage. Especially since those humble beginnings had nothing to do with computers. Mr. Hewlett and Mr. Packard were inventing test and measurement devices. The new program's focus should have been on HP's natural enemy.

IBM Is the Enemy

As you read earlier, number two has to attack number one and set itself up as the alternative. Sun Microsystems certainly is a strong competitor, but they are a specialist in UNIX workstations and servers. IBM is the one that HP must deal with to boost their share in corporate computing (where Fiorina is banking on huge growth). To go out after her stated goal of delivering E-business solutions, they need an anti-IBM strategy, not a me-too strategy. After all, IBM has a big services division and some brilliant

E-business advertising to back them up. What's Hewlett-Packard's angle? How can they present themselves as an alternative? Is Hewlett-Packard going to outinvent IBM? It's not likely, no matter how many little garages they throw at them.

When you're going against a larger competitor, you have to analyze their strength and avoid it. IBM's strength is that of their mainframe proprietary systems that have been placed in many large enterprise customers. In fact, many of these large-system sales drive much of IBM's fast growing systems-integration and consulting business. But the world is changing to internet-based open systems so mainframes are a slowly eroding business. Why do you think IBM rechristened the mainframe as an "enterprise server"? They are playing on customer interest in client/server systems.

This sets up an opportunity to exploit IBM's weakness in this growing category.

"World Leader in Open Enterprise Computing"

The trick is explain how Hewlett-Packard got to be number two in the marketplace. IBM did it with proprietary mainframe systems; HP did it with open client-server systems. And HP has the credentials to own this position. The last time I looked:

- HP is the No. 1 provider of open systems worldwide.
- HP is the No. 1 UNIX vendor in the world (the open operating system).
- HP has moved more companies to open systems than any other brand.

This sets up the opportunity to strengthen and build a services business to challenge IBM, Accenture, and EDS. They could rename their services business as Hewlett-Packard's Open Computing Services Organization. What their organization brings to a customer is helping an enterprise transition to the open systems world. Doing this might make more sense than Carly's efforts to buy the consulting arm of PriceWaterhouse Coopers for $16 billion.

That's because HP is in a perfect position to do the opposite of IBM, whose management never saw a computer system they didn't like. They can accentuate the negative.

The Key Benefit: Less Risk

Hewlett-Packard can make the point that the key benefit they bring to these enterprises is that of reducing risk. Their deep understanding of the "open" technology as well as HP's enormous experience sets up the Law of Candor: Admit a negative and the prospect will give you a positive.

The truth is that many service organizations overpromise and underdeliver. Also, many service organizations downplay the time and cost of downsizing. This has led to some very unhappy CEOs. For example, CSC Index, a consulting firm in Cambridge, Massachusetts, conducted a survey with the American Management Association of 376 CEOs. They found that roughly 50 percent of all technology projects fail to meet chief executives' expectations. This sets up an enormous opportunity for HP to:

- Talk about the dark side of downsizing.
- Talk about what you can't do in moving to open systems.
- Talk about new Internet services that avoid "hype," "overload," and "security."
- Talk about why "less risk" means Hewlett-Packard is a preferred vendor for complicated software systems such as SAP.

In short, it's the kind of stuff that IBM would never talk about. It's also the kind of stuff that fits HP's conservative image. And best of all, you don't have to go out and invent a lot of stuff to make this strategy work. Hewlett-Packard would be on its way to becoming a powerful alternative to IBM (the enemy).

That little exercise gives you a general sense of how knowing your competition can help you succeed while staying out of trouble. But here are a few more competitive guidelines.

Avoid a Competitor's Strength and Exploit Their Weakness

When a competitor is known for one thing, you have to be known for something else. Quite often, a competitor's built-in weakness is the something else that you can exploit. If McDonald's strength is that of being a little kids' place, Burger King can exploit that by being a grown-up kids' place. IBM is known for large proprietary computer systems. Hewlett-Packard can exploit that by offering open, distributed computer systems.

But remember, we're talking strength and weakness in the minds of the marketplace. Marketing is a battle of perceptions. What you're really doing is exploiting perceptions.

Always Be a Little Bit Paranoid about Competition

We're living in a world where everyone is after everyone's business. You have to realize that one of your competitors is probably in a meeting figuring out how to nail you in some way or another. You must constantly be gathering information on what your competitors are planning. This can come from an astute sales force or a friendly customer or from some research.

Never underestimate your competitor. In fact, you're safer if you overestimate them. AT&T, DEC, Levi's, and Crest are testimony to underestimating the kind of damage competitors can do even to market leaders.

Competitors Will Usually Get Better, If Pushed

Companies that figure they can exploit a sloppy competitor make big mistakes. They ridicule their product or service and say they can do things better. Then, lo and behold, their big competitor suddenly improves and that so-called advantage melts away.

Number two Avis did indeed try harder, but Hertz quickly improved their efforts. Then one day they ran a devastating ad with the headline, *For years, Avis has been telling you they are No. 2. Now we're going to tell you why.*

Then they went on to lay out all their improvements. Avis never quite recovered. Never build your program around your competitor's mistakes. They will correct them in short order.

When Business Is Threatened, Competitors Aren't Rational

Survival is a powerful instinct in life and in business. When threatened, all rationality goes out the window. I have a favorite story about this tendency.

A start-up company came up with a unique packaging system for baby carrots that produced a decided price advantage over the two big suppliers already in the business.

To get on the supermarket shelves, they entered the market not with better carrots but with a better price, which the established brands immediately matched. This only forced the new company to go lower, which once again was matched by their competitors.

When a board member asked the management of the start-up to predict what would happen, the management predicted that the two big companies would not continue to reduce their prices because it was "irrational." They were losing money because of their older packaging technology.

The board member called me about the prediction. I advised him that they would continue to be irrational until they forced this new upstart out of the market. Why would they make it easy for a new company that threatened their stable business?

At the next board meeting, the start-up company management was encouraged to sell their new manufacturing system to one of the established brands. Which they did for a nice profit.

So much for companies being rational.

Squash Your Smaller Competitors as Quickly as Possible

In war, the generals have an important maxim about being attacked:

> The best place to deal with an invading force is to get them in the water where they have the least maneuverability. Next, attack them on the beaches where they have limited maneuverability. But most of all, don't let them get inland where they can develop momentum.

So it is in business: You must move against your smaller competitors as soon as possible so they cannot develop legitimacy and momentum. General Motors hung back when the Germans and Japanese invaded the U.S. market with small cars. They felt they couldn't make any money on this type of car so they quickly rationalized their position by convincing themselves that Americans wanted big comfortable cars. Wrong.

Gillette, on the other hand, countered BIC's disposable razors with the twin-bladed disposable called Good News. They may not make much money on these razors (they love to get us by the blades), but today they dominate this category as well as the traditional and more profitable category of cartridge razors.

But you have to be careful here. No one squashed competition better than Microsoft. My advice: Keep squashing until you hear from the feds. Then apologize and back off a bit.

If You've Got a Bigger Competitor, Avoid Being Squashed

Here's the other side of the coin. How do you avoid a big competitor that has just taken my advice?

In two words, be careful.

The best strategy is to sneak up on a bigger competitor early on and never appear to be threatening. Slowly build your business and momentum in places where you're less visible. After you've got some size and momentum, you can step up and better deal with the bigger players.

Wal-Mart stores got their start in lightly populated C and D counties of the United States where their main competitors were mom and pop retailers. Only after they built size and momentum did they move into the heavily populated A and B counties where they confronted the other big mass merchandisers.

Southwest Airlines pursued a similar strategy of slowly building their route structure in nonhub airports and limited routes. They started in Texas, moved to the West Coast, then spread up into the Midwest, and now are working their way around the East. By the time the big airlines took them on, Southwest had real momentum. And Herb Kelleher maintained some real differences from his bigger competitors that kept his costs down: no food, no reservations, no hubs, and just one kind of plane. Now he runs Superbowl ads, is highly visible, and is kicking butt.

If You're Losing the Battle, Shift the Battlefield

A company that takes a licking will not keep ticking. (Only a Timex watch does that.) Even companies with deep pockets will suffer in this very competitive world. A better approach is to shift your efforts to a place where you can better take advantage of your strengths.

By manufacturing in the United States, Levi's couldn't compete on price with the me-too jeans manufacturers. By shifting to an authentic or original strategy, they could have played to their strength while making the case of paying a little more for the jeans. And it also would have given them time to shift manufacturing offshore.

Kellogg's is losing the battle with its current strategy. Shifting the focus to "real cereal" versus "processed cereal" puts the issue in a context that favors Kellogg's, a company that makes its cereal the old fashioned way.

You want to move the marketplace to a point where you can use your point of difference against your competitor instead of being hammered by your competitor's point of difference.

If a Bigger Competitor Is about to Attack, You Should Attack First

Finally, you must face reality about size and force. As in war, the bigger armies generally tend to overwhelm smaller armies. More people shooting at fewer people almost always results in a victory for the side with more people.

So if you're faced with a major attack, you must find a way to attack first if for no other reason than to keep your competitor distracted and off balance. If you don't, you will be overrun quickly and decisively.

That was exactly what faced DEC as IBM was readying its small computer attack with the PC. An early launch of a more powerful, minicomputer-based desktop machine would have dramatically slowed down IBM's penetration into the business market. It would have raised questions about whether IBM's PC was powerful and serious enough. Instead, by not attacking, DEC gave IBM time to improve the power and performance of these machines by introducing new generations (the XT and the AT).

In short order, DEC's decline was set in place.

A Tip

Managing in this highly competitive overcommunicated global economy is not easy. There are so many things to keep track of and so many variables in play that you can almost become dizzy trying to sort them all out. The way to avoid becoming dizzy is to do what the ballerinas do when they go into one of their high-speed pirouettes. As their head comes around in each turn, they stay focused on one thing or light in the audience. That's how they keep from getting dizzy.

The same goes for staying out of trouble. If you stay focused on your competition, you won't lose focus and wander off in a direction that could lead you into trouble.

CHAPTER
17

The Bigger They Are, the Harder to Manage

S ince we've been discussing all things "big" and the dangers of "growth," it is worth exploring whether that "desperate desire to grow" is truly worth all the effort.

When you start to study the subject of getting big, you can quickly come up with a stunning amount of research and analysis that seriously questions whether bigger is better. By the time I was finished, I began to wonder what in the world these CEOs were thinking about as they got trapped in the land of mergermania.

Let's start with the academics.

The Bigness Complex

In a detailed study, two economists produced a 400-page analysis that confronts the quintessential myth of corporate culture: that industrial giants in an organizational bigness are the handmaidens of economic efficiency. In a 1986 book entitled, *Bigness Complex* (Pantheon Books, 1986), they argue that the preoccupation with bigness is at the heart of the United States' economic decline.

A little hindsight shows that they miscalled our "economic decline." Quite the opposite occurred as we roared off into an amazing economic expansion. They also missed that these big companies have been falling apart on their own and we don't need any government policy to keep bad bigness things from happening. And they missed the small company explosion in high-tech land that helped propel our expansion.

As I've written earlier, you can't predict the future. But they did make some powerful points about "big."

Big Isn't More Efficient

After an intense amount of original and observed research, the authors concluded that conglomerate bigness seldom enhances, and more typically undermines, efficiency in production. They point to two studies: A classic 1956 study by Joe S. Bain and a much later study by F. M. Scherer that have these key findings:

1. Optimum plant sizes tend to be quite small relative to the national market.
2. Loss of production efficiency is surprisingly small in plants much smaller than those of optimal scale.
3. Substantial deconcentration could be effected while causing only slight scale economy sacrifices.

It's no wonder that big business has been replacing huge manufacturing complexes with new, smaller plants. Companies discovered that their people can't manage their way out of the problems created by size and complexity.

Big Doesn't Attack Itself

When a company is rich and successful, they don't want anything to change. IBM didn't want to see their mainframe world shift to small computers. General Motors didn't want to see their big car world shift to small cars.

As a result, inventions that undercut their main business are frowned on. Rare is the big successful company that says, "Hey that's a better idea. Let's dump our original idea." Instead, they quickly point out the flaws in this new idea. What they never take into consideration is that this new thing can be improved to a point where it can become what is called a disruptive technology or one that shifts the balance of power.

Market leaders have to be willing to attack themselves with a better idea. If they don't, someone else will.

Big Doesn't Organize Well

Economists do touch on the difficulties of organizing big companies, but to me, the best analysis of managing size came from a British anthropologist named Robin Dunbar. In an excellent book entitled *The Tipping Point* (Little, Brown & Co., 2000), Malcolm Gladwell introduces us to Dunbar, whose work revolved around what he called social capacity or how big a group we can run with and feel comfortable. His observation is that humans socialize in the largest group of primates because we are the only animals with brains large enough to handle the complexities of that social arrangement. His observation was that the figure of 150 seems to represent the maximum number of individuals with whom we can have a genuinely social relationship that goes with knowing who they are and how they relate to us.

Mr. Gladwell extracted from Dunbar's work the following observation that gets to the heart of being too big:

At a bigger size you have to impose complicated hierarchies and rules and regulations and formal measures to try to command loyalty and cohesion. But below 150, Dunbar argues, it is possible to achieve these same goals informally: "At this size orders can be implemented and unruly behavior controlled on the basis of personal loyalties and direct man-to-man contacts with larger groups, this becomes impossible."

Personal Agenda

What Mr. Dunbar never envisioned was what happens in big companies. What advanced primates all have is called a reflex personal agenda. It goes like this: When faced with a decision that could be best for the company versus one that could be best for the individual, a large percentage of the time a human primate will opt for the decision that betters his or her career. Another expression of this is "making your mark."

In all my years in the business, I've never seen a marketing person come into a new assignment, look around, and say, "Things look pretty good. Let's not touch a thing." On the contrary, all red-blooded marketing people want to get in there and start improving things. They want to make their mark. Just sitting there wouldn't feel right. When a company has offices full of people, you've got to expect endless tinkering with a brand. It's how they keep from getting bored.

It's also how brands get in trouble. The more people you have, the more difficult it is to manage them.

Big by Merger Can Be Trouble

At the turn of the twentieth century, a great number of corporate giants were created: General Electric (a combination of 8 firms controlling 90 percent of the market); Du Pont (64 firms controlling

70 percent); Nabisco (27 firms, 70 percent); Otis Elevator (6 firms, 65 percent); International Paper (24 firms, 60 percent).

But those days are over. The past 30 years are strewn with failures: the 1970s' conglomerates often failed to produce promised profits and the 1980s' buyouts often reduced efficiency and saddled companies with more debt than they could repay. And merging distinct corporations sometimes takes longer than expected which only gives our friends on Wall Street high anxiety.

If you have doubts about this, consider the following rundown of the biggest turkeys to emerge from the recent wave of deal mania. It comes from an article in *Business Week* aptly named, "Let's Talk Turkeys":

1996

Union Pacific and Southern Pacific
The $4 billion deal was to have created a
"seamless" rail network from the
Midwest to the West Coast. The reality
was complete gridlock.

1997

NFS and CUC International
This $14 billion deal to create Cendant
was intended to build a marketing
powerhouse. But accounting
irregularities at CUC sent Cendant's share
price down 46 percent in one day and
triggered a federal probe.

1998

Conseco and Green Tree Financial
With the $7.6 billion acquisition of
lender Green Tree, insurer Conseco
foresaw a bonanza. But Green Tree was
hit by huge charges on bad loans.

1999

Aetna and Prudential Healthcare
Aetna hoped that the $1 billion deal
would make it the No. 1 HMO. But Pru
and a string of troubled mergers led to
the ouster of Aetna's CEO. Now, the
company is breaking in two.

AT&T
Its back-to-back deals for TCI and MediaOne
for a combined $90 billion backfired on CEO
C. Michael Armstrong. He tried to sell
consumers on packaged telecom services, but
AT&T's core businesses dried up. Now, with
its shares in the tank, AT&T is breaking up again.

Mattel and Learning Co.
Mattel hoped to break into the CD-ROM
game market with the $3.5 billion purchase.
But then the Internet caught on, drying up
the CD-ROM market. Mattel's stock
crashed, and CEO Jill E. Barad was ousted.

Allied Signal and Honeywell
Allied Signal hoped to combine its
efficiency with Honeywell's product
innovation. Instead, the $14 billion
combo got hit by rising oil prices, a
plunging euro, and management problems.

Federated Department Stores and Fingerhut
Federated paid $1.7 billion to apply
Fingerhut's direct-marketing skills to its
Macy's and Bloomingdale's units. But
Fingerhut's focus on low-end consumers
led to huge write-offs.

McKesson and HBO
The $12 billion merger of No. 1 drug
wholesaler McKesson and medical software
maker HBO & Co. ran into a buzz saw.
Auditors uncovered an accounting scandal
at HBO leading to resignations and criminal
charges. McKesson shares are off 47 percent
for the year.

(December 11, 2000)

Putting small businesses in the same business together to get big can make some sense. Putting big businesses together that are in different businesses is the road to big trouble.

Why Things Go Wrong

Studies have shown that a large percentage of mergers underperform their grand predictions of success. Two large companies that join together spend so much time on operational integration that they end up running on the fumes of past glory and brand name. What you rarely see are new ideas or innovation. What's behind the merger of Mobil and Exxon? As best I can figure, it's a bunch of accountants and efficiency experts figuring out how to cut costs, gain market share, and boost their stock price.

Immense resources and big brand names rarely guarantee innovation. More often, all that tradition and bureaucracy get in the way of any radical thinking.

The Problems Multiply

What also comes with a big merger are double or triple the number of employees, products, shareholders, and customers. Managing all this becomes exceptionally difficult. Pretty soon, there are endless meetings about logos, cutting head counts, closing offices, selling off businesses, and figuring out how to put the right spin on all this to customers.

Next up are the problems with keeping the company's best people from taking their egos elsewhere. Pecking orders get disrupted. Everyone's trying to figure out who is up, who is down, and who is out.

The actual business at hand is buried in a flurry of rumors and time spent looking for a new job.

But what tops all the problems is what they call culture clash or bringing together two highly complex, large, and not necessarily like-minded companies. Culture is "the way we do things around here." This includes participation in decision making, performance rewards, risk tolerance, and quality and cost orientation. All this leads to, at great expense, a great deal of touchy-feely communication and integration seminars. Team building and sensitivity training become the rage, and change management consultants ride into town.

That's what happens in U.S. mergers. When you have global mergers such as the likes of DaimlerChrysler, all that new age stuff goes out the window. Can a German carmaker ever integrate with the likes of a Detroit carmaker? Not likely. You know what those Mercedes engineers think of those Chrysler engineers? Not much. No change management consultants will change those attitudes.

Stall Points

If all that history and analysis wasn't enough to throw cold water on getting big, I came across a Washington, D.C., organization called the Corporate Strategy Board. They, in association with, of all corporations, Hewlett-Packard, developed a study on the theoretical limits to growth. They studied corporate "stall experiences" over four decades and concluded that big is indeed very difficult to manage for growth. The numbers are hard to argue with. A $40 million company needs only $8 million to grow 20 percent. A $4 billion company needs $800 million. Very few new markets are that large. This means that the larger and more successful a company is, the more difficult it will become to maintain that pace.

Interestingly, 83 percent of the root causes for company stall points were controllable. Either strategic factors or organizational factors led to trouble. Translation: It's easy to make management mistakes with giant corporations—the bigger they are, the harder to manage.

This study actually came up with a ceiling or cloud level where companies probably run into problems as they climb. The number is about $30 billion in sales. Now for a stunning statistic: By 1999, the annual revenue of the 50 largest public companies in the United States was about $50.8 billion. That means we have a couple of squadrons of behemoths flying in the clouds and headed for stalls of one kind or another. (Look out on the ground.)

CEOs Struggling to Keep Pace

All this growth and size has left a number of mega-companies struggling. DaimlerChrysler is cutting 26,000 jobs at Chrysler. Bank of America Corporation and Bank One merged and have had to struggle with high costs. WorldCom acquired MCI and is now busy undoing much of the merger.

It's no wonder that the *Wall Street Journal* wrote an excellent article on CEOs struggling with bigness. To them, running a company has taken on a "new kind of complexity and a new degree of turmoil." The article summed up the problems neatly:

> Capital whips around the globe, economics gyrate and consumer tastes turn on a drive. Information travels almost instantly, be it an earnings forecast or a nasty rumor. Dumb moves or stumbles are subject to much greater scrutiny. Decisions must be made quickly, with limited information. Vastly expanded overseas operations can make simple every day functions, like communicating with employees, increasingly difficult.

It would appear that today's CEO isn't getting much sleep.

Keeping in Touch

What many CEOs are doing is shifting their energies to the new technologies. One CEO sends periodic e-mails to 30,000 employees asking for feedback. (Help, I'm up to my waist in printouts!) Another has regular videoconferences where he carefully delivers the same speech over and over as not to send mixed messages. (Help, I'm being bored to death by the same speech!) Yet another keeps an Internet connection on all day, reads six daily newspapers, and skims an array of magazines from around the world. (Help, I'm going blind from having to read so much!) And then there's the endless plane travel where a CEO can easily log over 150,000 miles a year. (Help, my body doesn't know what time it is any more!)

But what I really found alarming was the growing need to spend more and more time on public relations and investor relations. One CEO spends a day each week doing this kind of stuff. His reason, "Large investors want access permanently. It has become accepted that you will always talk to major shareholders."

This means someone else has to run the day-to-day business.

Well, there you have it; the CEOs of these big companies haven't enough time to get involved in some of those important decisions that come back to bite them later. ("I'd like to spend more time on this, but I have to call back a big investor.")

It's no wonder the corporate mortality rate of CEOs is on the rise.

CHAPTER

18

Trouble Begins and Ends with the CEO

I n the old days, your big company CEO was far behind the firing line. When things went bad, there were people to be blamed and asked to leave. But today, it's a different story. The buck stops at the office of the CEO.

Toward the latter part of 2000, an executive employment firm estimated that 350 chief executives in the United States had left their jobs. Among them were some big names from big companies having trouble. They didn't last very many months on the job. Take a look: Richard McGinn (36 months at Lucent), John McDonough (35 months at Newell Rubbermaid), Dale Morrison (33 months at Campbell Soup), Michael Howley (17 months at Gillette), Durk Jager (17 months at Procter & Gamble), and Lloyd Ward (15 months at Maytag).

This kind of turnover was unheard of in the past. After all, Jack Welch has survived the disastrous "factory of the future" fiasco that sank without a trace in a sea of technical snafus and erroneous projections of customer demand. The late Roberto Goizueta of Coca-Cola survived the New Coke disaster, which has become the poster product of bad ideas.

Today, those executives would have been toast because there appears to be zero forgiveness for mistakes. You screw up and you're dead. As mentioned, boards have gotten good at firing if not fixing problems before they occur. And also, there is a lot more intensity in absolutely hitting the numbers 100 percent. It's not a range anymore, it's a specific number. And as major businesses do multiple acquisitions, they are hard things to pull together; something always shows up to bite CEOs in the balance sheet.

Mm, Mm, Bad

What happened at Campbell Soup is instructive. David Johnson took charge of this venerable soup company in 1990. Johnson did what Jack Welch did early in his reign at GE. He carved costs out of an old-line operation and raised prices where he could. Campbell's stock price tripled during his tenure powered by a jump in net profit margins. That Johnson was unable to boost the soup maker's anemic rate of revenue growth was disappointing but not surprising. Soup is soup. It's been around a long time and people get bored eating the same thing. Besides, all that fast food out there is changing people's eating habits. ("Let's send out for a pizza.")

Then Campbell Soup brought in Dale Morrison from PepsiCo Inc. In 1997, he got the top job and thus the Wall Street spotlight. Morrison realized that there wasn't much more fat to trim. Raising prices further was a hazardous option in a very competitive market. So he dedicated himself to selling more soup, more Pepperidge Farm cookies, V8 Juice, and Godiva chocolates. That's all fine if you can do it. But he made a fatal mistake by promising Wall Street 8 percent to 10 percent annual growth and double-digit growth in earnings per share. It never happened, and in no time Mr. Morrison was toast.

It's Not about "the Numbers"

If you live by the numbers, you can die by the numbers. CEOs that look at their jobs purely in the context of pushing the troops to make their forecasts are risking not only their jobs but the health of the organization. Nothing demonstrates this more than the sad saga of Richard McGinn. He was the CEO of Lucent Technologies and had turned the former equipment-making arm of AT&T into a Wall Street star by increasing sales at a double-digit pace.

But nothing goes up forever and in 2000 Lucent missed its numbers twice. So the pressure was on the sales troops. From numerous reports in the business press, McGinn's message was to do deals, no holds barred. According to the press, the company promised its customers a host of discounts, one-time credits, and other incentives certain to eat into future sales. When they badly missed their numbers again, all hell broke loose and Mr. McGinn bit the dust. The stock plunged and Lucent's future has been put in some doubt. As I said earlier, you can die by being too focused on the numbers.

First, the Bad News

There are no superheroes and top executives have to realize that the impossible is impossible, no matter how hard you push the troops.

Jack Welch types are an anomaly. Today's new CEOs have no chance to match Welch's longevity because there is no more difficult task than the one they are likely to face: transforming a core business threatened by a new technology. George Fisher tried that at Kodak and it doesn't appear that they will find much happiness in the digital age. And if CEOs get trapped in the great expectations of future growth, they will most probably fail.

What's at the heart of all this is that, in many instances, big company CEOs are barely in control of their company's fate, much less their own. There is a growing legion of competitors coming at them from every corner of the globe. Technologies are ever changing. The pace of change is faster. It is increasingly difficult for CEOs to digest the flood of information out there and make the right choices.

Now for the Good News

But a CEO can have a future.

The trick to surviving out there is not to stare at the balance sheet but simply to know where you must go to find success in a market. That's because no one can follow you (the board, your managers, your employees) if you don't know where you're headed.

Many years ago in a book called *The Peter Principle*, authors Peter and Hull made this observation: "Most hierarchies are nowadays so cumbered with rules and traditions, and so bound in by public laws, that even high employees do not have to lead anyone anywhere, in the sense of pointing out the direction and setting the pace. They simply follow precedents, obey regulations, and move at the head of the crowd. Such employees lead only in the sense that the carved wooden figurehead leads the ship."

A Book to Guide You?

Perhaps this pessimistic view of leadership skills has led to the explosion of hundreds of books dealing with leadership (most of them downright silly). There's advice on whom to emulate (Attila the Hun), what to achieve (inner peace), what to study (failure), what to strive for (charisma), whether to delegate (sometimes), whether to collaborate (maybe), America's secret leaders (women), the personal qualities of leadership (having integrity), how to achieve credibility (be credible), how to be an authentic leader (find the leader within), and the nine natural laws of leadership (don't even ask). In fact, there are more than 3,000 books in print with the word "leader" in the title.

How to be an effective leader isn't worth a whole book. The fabled management guru, Peter Drucker, gets it into a few sentences: "The foundation of effective leadership is thinking through the organization's mission, defining it and establishing it, clearly and visibly. The leader sets the goals, sets the priorities, and sets and maintains the standards."

How do you find the proper direction? To become a great strategist, you have to put your mind in the mud of the marketplace. You have to find your inspiration down at the front, in the ebb and flow of the great marketing battles taking place in the mind of the prospect.

It's about Perceptions

If there's one lesson to take out of this book, it is this: *Success or failure are all about perceptual problems and opportunities in the marketplace. And it's all about understanding that the mind of the customer is where you win and lose.*

You cannot be swayed by those wonderful presentations by your executives on how your company can make a better product or leverage your better distribution or your better sales force to get into the marketplace. You have to stay focused on the mind of the prospect. Minds are difficult if not impossible to change. And if your executives say it can be done, don't believe them. The more you understand the minds of your customers or prospects, the less likely you will get into trouble.

I once asked one of the ex-CEOs of General Motors if he ever questioned the proliferation of models that eventually destroyed the meaning of the company's brands (he was a financial man with lit-tle background in marketing).

That question caused him to stop and ponder for a few seconds. His response: "No, but I do recall thinking that it was getting a little confusing." His concern was absolutely correct but he failed to act on his instincts. His assumption was that his executives knew what they were doing. This turned out to be a false assumption. But it took a number of years for this mistake to be felt at General Motors. Today, thanks to intense competition, mistakes are felt in a matter of months, not years. That's why marketing is too important to turn over to an underling. To survive, a CEO has to assume the final responsibility for what gets taken to the marketplace. After all, your job is on the line.

I once said just that to the head of a very large division in a very large company. While he acknowledged the importance of being involved, he expressed his concern about undercutting the respon-sibility of those middle-level executives in charge. Well, you have to put those concerns aside if you want to stay out of trouble.

It's about Knowing What's Up

The unpretentious Sam Walton traveled to the front lines of every one of his Wal-Mart stores throughout his life. He even spent time in the middle of the night on the loading docks, talking with the crews.

Unlike "Mister Sam," many chief executives tend to lose touch. The bigger the company, the more likely it is that the chief execu-tive has lost touch with the front lines. This might be the single most important factor in CEOs' mistakes. How do you know what is really happening? How do you get around the propensity of mid-dle management to tell you what they think you want to hear? How do you get the bad news as well as the good?

If you don't get the bad news directly, bad ideas can flourish in-stead of being killed.

One possibility of finding out what's really going on is "going in disguise" or poking around unannounced. This would be especially useful at the distributor or retail level. The reason: To get honest opinions of what's happening.

The members of the sales force, if you have one, are a critical element in the equation. The trick is how to get a good, honest evaluation of the competition out of them. The best thing you can do is to praise honest information. Once the word gets around that a CEO prizes honesty and reality, a lot of useful information will be forthcoming.

It's about Thinking Long-Term

Let's just say you've focused on your competitors and figured out their strengths and weaknesses in the mind. You have searched out the one attribute or differentiating idea that will work in the mental battleground.

Then you have focused all your efforts to develop a coherent strategy to exploit that idea. And you have been willing to make the changes inside the organization to exploit the opportunities on the outside.

Now you must be willing to take the time to let that strategy develop. Marketing moves take time to develop so you must—in the face of pressure from Wall Street, the board, and your employees—be willing to stay the course. Nothing demonstrates this better than the Lotus Development Corporation, the company that invented the spreadsheet for the PC.

They were overrun by Microsoft with their version of the spreadsheet, Excel for Windows. Since Microsoft invented Windows and Lotus was late with their version of a Windows spreadsheet, Lotus was in deep trouble. Jim Manzi, then the CEO, decided to shift the battlefield. To him, the future of the brand had to be "Groupware" because they had in early stages a product called "Notes," which was the first successful Groupware program (software designed for groups or networks for computers as opposed to software for individual PCs). So Groupware became the focus as Jim Manzi began the process of building and supporting the Notes/Groupware business.

It's about Hanging in There

Getting to where Lotus is today took an enormous effort. When asked about this effort of changing focus, Jim Manzi summed it up as a "brutal process." Here is the story he told me in his own words:

> The spreadsheet was the center of gravity at Lotus. It once represented 70 percent of our business. It was our "mainframe" business, so to speak. But Microsoft and Windows really put a big hole in our future.
>
> In the early nineties I felt Notes was the best future we had. Unfortunately, not everyone in the company felt that way. Many wanted to just continue to improve the spreadsheet. During one difficult period, twelve VPs left the company.
>
> They didn't see the future the way I did.
>
> All this, plus the ongoing investment in this product, didn't go unnoticed by our Board of Directors. Keeping them on the Notes bandwagon required telling the story over and over, maintaining perspective, and building relationships both inside and outside the company. Once the Board loses that vision of the future, your problems magnify.
>
> Luckily the numbers started to get better and people started to get more comfortable with an investment that is closing in on $500 million.

Jim Manzi certainly knew where he was going. The end of the story was a happy one. IBM bought the company for $3.5 billion and has since made Lotus one of its cornerstones in their software efforts with their enterprise customers. Lotus was in big trouble but a bold, long-term effort bailed them out of a potentially fatal problem.

The Beginning and the End

If one theme runs through this book, it is that CEOs often make bad decisions leading to big trouble. They either do things that cause problems or don't do things that could have avoided problems.

And when danger looms, the CEO is probably the only person who can effectively take the company out of harm's way.

He or she is indeed the captain of the ship. And every CEO should have a plaque on the wall that reads:

♦REMEMBER THE TITANIC.♦

INDEX

"Consumer" Perceptions"

Modules

- Share/ Rel Profit - who
- Cons: relationship w/
  Product - Depth
  involvement etc

- "Width" of brand -
  Some line ext OK-
  check w/ consumer

- Positioning/Differentiation
  -- Compet.